W9-BDW-581

Praise for *Key Business Analytics*

'Why was this book not written earlier? Key Business Analytics *is an excellent compendium of the analysis tools you really need, explained in a way that is practical and rigorous.'*

ROBERT SHAW, HONORARY PROFESSOR OF MARKETING ANALYTICS, CASS
BUSINESS SCHOOL

'Many business and technology leaders are aware of the opportunities advanced analytics can bring to their businesses but struggle to define how exactly value is going to be generated. Bernard Marr has produced a book that fills a substantial gap in the analytics literature. He gives, with great detail, insights as to how virtually any business can benefit from modern analytics. This book must be a reference to practitioners and managers, as well as technologists.'

DR AHMED KHAMASSI, GLOBAL HEAD OF INSIGHTS, WIPRO DIGITAL

'This book demystifies analytics and provides a practical guide for any business professional. Bernard makes it clear which methods and processes are applicable to a wide range of business needs.'

RICH CLAYTON, VICE PRESIDENT, BUSINESS ANALYTICS, ORACLE

'This book is a must-have for anyone trying to navigate the data analytics landscape. Thoughtfully organised and full of practical, real-life cases, this handy reference will help you cut through the big data hype and understand the many ways that analytics can benefit your business. Whether you are new to analytics or a big data guru, this book should be on your desk.'

SCOTT ETKIN, WRITER, JOURNALIST AND EDITOR, DATA INFORMED

'While early adopters are busy implementing business analytics solutions, a majority of business leaders are just beginning their analytics focus and need a jargon-free reference guide. Bernard Marr's book is this guide. He provides readers with a non-technical, high-level overview of seven critical areas of analytics. He defines terminology, types of analytics and business areas that can quickly see benefit from analytics. Each area is practical and guides managers towards quick ways to get up to speed and join the conversation. I highly recommend this book for managers feeling excluded from today's business analytics conversation.'

GRETA ROBERTS, CEO, TALENT ANALYTICS, CORP.

'Straightforward, engaging and entirely practical – Bernard Marr provides a comprehensive toolkit to rigorously analyse all aspects of your business.'

DR SIMON BOUCHER, CHIEF EXECUTIVE, IRISH MANAGEMENT INSTITUTE

'An essential reference guide which demystifies the complexity surrounding analytical techniques. This book offers practical examples and advice on where to implement data analytics for maximum return.'

LEIGH BATES, DIRECTOR, ADVANCED RISK AND COMPLIANCE ANALYTICS, PRICEWATERHOUSECOOPERS LLP

'Marr's new book Key Business Analytics is a must read for any professional who wants to stay current. The explanations are clear, concise and will bring you up to date in the field of business analytics and big data.'

VLADIMIR MELNIK, DIRECTOR, DATA AND ANALYTICS, ACCENTURE/AVANADE

Key Business Analytics

PEARSON

At Pearson, we believe in learning – all kinds of learning for all kinds of people. Whether it's at home, in the classroom or in the workplace, learning is the key to improving our life chances.

That's why we're working with leading authors to bring you the latest thinking and best practices, so you can get better at the things that are important to you. You can learn on the page or on the move, and with content that's always crafted to help you understand quickly and apply what you've learned.

If you want to upgrade your personal skills or accelerate your career, become a more effective leader or more powerful communicator, discover new opportunities or simply find more inspiration, we can help you make progress in your work and life.

Pearson is the world's leading learning company. Our portfolio includes the Financial Times and our education business, Pearson International.

Every day our work helps learning flourish, and wherever learning flourishes, so do people.

To learn more, please visit us at **www.pearson.com/uk**

The Financial Times

With a worldwide network of highly respected journalists, *The Financial Times* provides global business news, insightful opinion and expert analysis of business, finance and politics. With over 500 journalists reporting from 50 countries worldwide, our in-depth coverage of international news is objectively reported and analysed from an independent, global perspective.

To find out more, visit **www.ft.com/pearsonoffer/**

About the author

Bernard Marr is a bestselling business author, keynote speaker and consultant in big data, analytics and enterprise performance. As the founder and CEO of the Advanced Performance Institute, he is one of the world's most highly respected thought leaders when it comes to data in business. He regularly advises companies and government organisations on how to gain better insights from their data.

Bernard is a frequent contributor to the World Economic Forum and Forbes, and is acknowledged by LinkedIn as one of the world's top 50 business influencers.

In his consulting work he helps companies develop KPIs and data sets to find answers to their most important business questions. Companies and organisations he has advised include: Accenture, AllianceBoots, Astra Zeneca, Bank of England, Bank of Ireland, Barclays, BP, DHL, Fujitsu, Gartner, the Home Office, HSBC, IBM, Mars, the Ministry of Defence, Microsoft, Oracle, the NHS, Orange, the Royal Air Force, SAP, Shell, Tetley, T-Mobile, Toyota, as well as the UN and many others.

Other recent books by Bernard include: *Big Data: Using Smart Big Data*; *Analytics and Metrics to Make Better Decisions and Improve Performance*; *Key Performance Indicators: The 75 Measures Every Manager Needs To Know*; and *The Intelligent Company*.

If you would like to talk to Bernard about any consulting, training or speaking engagement then you can contact him at www.ap-institute.com or via email at bernard.marr@ap-institute.com

You can follow @bernardmarr on Twitter, where he regularly shares his ideas, and also connect with him on LinkedIn, where he writes a regular blog.

Introduction

Analytics is something every business needs to stay competitive in today's data-filled world. Every manager needs to at least understand the basics of analytics and when and where to apply it. This is where this book comes in: it provides a complete roadmap of the key areas where analytics can be used in business as well as an overview of key analytics techniques. The book will help you to understand some of the most important analytics techniques, which areas in business to apply them and how to get the data to run the analytics.

It is impossible to open a leadership or management journal without reading something on the explosion of 'big data', 'analytics', 'business intelligence (BI)', 'knowledge management', 'data mining', 'data discovery' or 'decision support'.

There is often a great deal of confusion around these terms and often they are used synonymously and interchangeably, which can often amplify the confusion. This book is designed to eliminate some of that confusion and help you understand the crux of analytics so you can ignore the buzz words and hype and appreciate what it is and why it's a vital component of modern business. And perhaps most importantly you will become familiar with the various key analytic tools available to you and when and why you might use them.

There is a great deal of interest in this area because it promises to unlock commercially relevant insights that can potentially be used to uncover new markets, new niche audiences within markets and areas for future research and development. Highly publicised stories and business case studies from data gods like Target, Walmart, Amazon, Facebook and Google can leave normal business leaders feeling vulnerable and overwhelmed – unsure of where to start or what to do in order to 'catch up'. The simple fact is that for most businesses it's impossible to reach those lofty data analytic heights, but that doesn't mean analytics is only for the big guns.

Nothing could be further from the truth. Analytics can improve performance in every business regardless of size but in order for it to deliver its promise we first need to understand it and dispel some of the fear around it – and that's where this book comes in.

In essence, analytics is about data and how we can use it to improve business success and performance. Clearly this concept is not new, business leaders and senior executives have been using past performance and business data for decades to help decide strategy and alter course when necessary. But what *is* new is our ever-expanding definition of what data is and the technological advances that allow us to store, analyse and extract value from data that was previously impossible.

The raw material – data

The raw material of this insight extraction process is data – whether that is traditional data or 'big data'. Currently the term 'big data' is used to describe the fact that everything we do, say, write, visit or buy leaves a digital trace, or it soon will, and the resulting data can then be used by us and others to gain new insights and improve results. Although the term 'big data' will probably disappear as 'big data' becomes plain old data, it is currently considered 'Big' because of 4 Vs:

- **Volume** – relating to the vast amounts of data that are being generated every second not least because of our love affair with smart technology and constant connectivity.

- **Velocity** – relating to the speed at which new data is generated and moves around the world. For example, fraud detection analytics tracks millions of credit card transactions for unusual patterns in almost real time.

- **Variety** – relating to the increasingly different types of data that are being generated from financial data to social media feeds, to photos to sensor data, to video footage to voice recordings.

- **Veracity** – relating to the messiness of the data being generated – just think of Twitter posts with hash tags, abbreviations, typos, text language and colloquial speech.

Used effectively the 4 Vs can also deliver the 5th V – **Value**. And that's what analytics is really all about – the use of data to deliver value. And analytics allows us to derive value by answering four key questions:

1. What happened?
2. Why did it happen?
3. What's happening now?
4. What might happen in the future?

Clearly these are important questions to know the answers to and analytics makes it possible. The easiest way to think about business analytics is that it is the process by which you take the raw material (data) and convert it into commercially relevant insights (analytics) that can inform business, improve performance and guide strategy (business intelligence).

Of course the validity and accuracy of that process depends on how clear you are about the key strategic questions you are seeking to answer *and* the quality of the data you use to answer those questions. So before we dive into the various key analytics let's step back and get really clear about the types and formats of data that can now be analysed.

Data types and format

When it comes to data there are a few key distinctions that are important to understand. Data is either structured, semi-structured or unstructured, and it is sourced from either inside your business or outside your business.

Structured data is data that is highly organised and located in a fixed field within a defined record or file. This includes data contained in relational databases or spreadsheets. Structured data is easy to input, easy to store and easy to analyse because it follows rules and is often accessed using Structured Query Language (SQL). While SQL represented a huge improvement over paper-based data storage and analysis not everything in business fits neatly into a predefined field and that's where semi-structured and unstructured data comes in.

It is estimated that 80 per cent of business-relevant information originates in unstructured or semi-structured data. And essentially it's everything else that can't be easily inserted into fields, rows or columns. It is often text heavy but may also contain dates, numbers and different types of data such as images or audio files.

Semi-structured data is a hybrid of unstructured and structured. This is data that may have some structure that can be used for analysis but large chunks are unstructured. For instance, a LinkedIn post can be categorised by author, date or length but the content is generally unstructured. Likewise, word processing software includes metadata detailing the author's name, when it was created and amended but the content of the document is still unstructured.

Of course the source of data is also important because most businesses are already data rich. The problem is they are insight poor and don't often know how to use the data they have, never mind utilise the treasure trove of external data that also exists. As a rule of thumb, internal data is usually easier and cheaper to access because it is owned and controlled by the business. This might include financial records, customer feedback, transaction history, employee surveys, HR data, etc.

External data as the name would suggest is any data that exists outside your business which is held either publicly or privately by another organisation. If data is public then you can collect it for free, pay a third party for it or hire a third party to collect it for you. Private data is usually something you would need to source and pay for from another business or third party data supplier. External data might include weather data, social media profile data, trend data or government-held data such as census information.

	Structured	Semi-Structured	Unstructured
Internal	• Point of sale • Financial data • Customer data • HR records	• Photos or graphics with tags or categories • Videos with tags or categories • Email	• Website • Text files • Photos • Audio • Social media
External	• Market research • GPS position data • Sensor data • Weather data	• Tagged photos • Organised graphics • Tagged videos • Categorised text	• Website • Text files • Photos • Audio • Social media

It is the explosion in semi-structured and unstructured data along with the technological capacity to store and analyse that data that now makes analytics so exciting. We now have the capability to analyse a variety of formats including:

- Images
- Text
- Numbers
- Video
- Audio
- Sensor data.

How to use this book

The best way to use this book would be to read about the key analytics that jump out at you or appear more interesting. Consider what areas in your business you are keen to understand more about and focus on those key analytic sections first.

If, for example, you really want to know more about your customers, what they like or dislike, how they are behaving, how their buying behaviour is changing, etc., then start with the customer analytics. If, on the other hand, you are interested in learning more about your market and how that is changing, then perhaps you should start with the market analytics.

The book's short-chapter structure means it is easy to flick back and forwards to whichever section you are more interested in, helping you to match your appreciation of analytics to your current need. Use the book as an essential reference guide that allows you to look up the key analytics you want to understand and then just jump in and test some techniques out.

Who is this book for?

This book is aimed at anyone in business that would like to better understand what analytics could offer. It is not a technical book on how to do advanced statistics and it would be impossible to cover so many different analytics techniques in just one book. This book is about providing a general understanding of the field and the ways analytics can be applied in any business. It will enable managers to engage in a more informed discussion about analytics and will help them make strategic decisions about where and how to apply it in practice.

The seven parts of this book

In the first part of the book I will explore the bare analytics to provide an overview of the most important types of analytics tools and approaches used in business today. In Part Two I look at the different analytics input tools and how best to find the data for your analytics. Parts Three–Six will then look at the different business functions and some of the most important applications of analytics within them: Part Three looks at financial analytics, Part Four at market analytics, Part Five explores customer analytics and Part Six looks at how you can apply analytics in HR and people areas. The final Part Seven explores analytics in operations and business processes.

[PART ONE]

Bare analytics

Business experiments/ experimental design/ AB testing

1

What is it?

Business experiments, experimental design and AB testing are all techniques for testing the validity of something – be that a strategic hypothesis, new product packaging or a marketing approach.

Business experiments tend to be the blanket term for this type of testing in business; experimental design is testing that occurs in product development; while AB testing is the term applied to tests that occur in marketing activity. Regardless of the term the principle goal in this type of testing is to extract the maximum amount of unbiased information regarding the various factors being tested so that the best course of action can be determined before implementation.

TV shows run this type of testing when they create a 'pilot' show to gauge audience reaction and interest before spending a huge amount of time, money and effort creating the whole series. These analytics tools are the same for business.

When do I use it?

In order to grow and develop as a business you need to innovate and take a few risks now and then. But innovation, product or service development or strategic changes can backfire because of faulty assumptions or information or your customers may simply not react the way you expect. Some sort of business experiment can help to reduce that risk considerably.

It should be used if you have two or more options to decide between and getting it wrong would pose a serious problem for your business. Running a test between the various options on a smaller, more manageable scale can allow you to work out which one is likely to yield the best results.

Plus the feedback from the experiments can help you to further refine and improve the winning option making it even more effective.

What business questions is it helping me to answer?

In essence, business experimentation can help you to decide which option to get behind when you are faced with one or more choices. For instance, it can help you to answer:

- Which of these options will increase sales?
- Which of these products should we focus on releasing first?
- Which of these products do our customers prefer?
- Which marketing campaign produces the highest response rate?
- Which recruitment channels are most effective?

How do I use it?

The detail will depend on what methodology you use and what you are trying to achieve but the basic process, outlined by analytics expert Thomas H. Davenport, is essentially the same:

1 Create a hypothesis.
2 Design the experiment.
3 Run the experiment.
4 Analyse results and follow up.

Create a hypothesis

Consider what it is you are testing and create a hypothesis around that outcome. For example, you might be keen to test changes to your product packaging to see how or if it affects sales. Chances are you already have an idea about how the test will work out – that's your hypothesis. So in this case your hypothesis might be, 'I believe that less packaging on our products will be appealing to our customers and increase sales'; or, 'I don't think changes in the packaging will influence sales at all.'

Perhaps you want to refresh your website but you're not exactly sure what you should change and what you should leave the same. So you decide to test it and your hypothesis is, 'Moving the "buy now" button from the bottom left to the top right will increase sales.'

When you are creating your hypothesis make sure:

- Whatever you are testing can be accurately measured for 'better'/'worse' or 'pass'/'fail' otherwise it's pointless.
- The test fits the team's or business's overall strategy and values? Never run a test that could damage your reputation even with a small group of people.
- The test will add value to your business.

Part of this stage is figuring out how you will measure your hypothesis so you need to know what success looks like. So in our earlier examples, the test around packaging will have been proven successful if the product with less packaging yields more sales than the standard packaging, and the website redesign test will be considered successful if moving the 'buy now' button generates more sales.

Design the experiment

Next you need to consider how to conduct the experiment as cost-effectively as possible and decide how long the experiment will take.

Some experiments are easier to design than others. If you are making a change to a product or service then you simply assess results prior to the change, make the change and then assess results after the change, comparing the two results. If, however, you are testing a modification to an existing product or existing marketing campaign then you need to ensure you can accurately measure the impact of the change and compare like with like. For example, if you were testing modifications to a product, you couldn't test the standard product against the modified product with five modifications because you wouldn't know which modifications were making the impact. This is where AB testing comes in because it allows you to test version A against version B where version B has only one modification; that way you know with a high degree of certainty that any difference in result is due to the single modification.

Only test one aspect at a time and where possible keep your experiments as simple as possible. This is not only to maintain accuracy over the results, but generally speaking the more complex the test the more expensive the test.

Run the experiment

Make sure you tell people about the experiment – especially those that will be affected by it. Make sure people understand why you are running the experiment and that they have plenty of advance warning.

Once the experiment is live simply monitor what's happening to make sure nothing has happened during the test period that could distort results. For example, if you are testing a product with less packaging and that product runs out for four days in the middle of the test, if you don't know about that from dispatch then you could assume that the product did not sell as well as the alternative. The truth, however, is that customers couldn't actually buy it for four days!

Analyse results and follow up

The only purpose of doing the experiment was to test your hypothesis and use the results to guide your decision making, so, as soon as the experiment is over, analyse the results thoroughly.

Compare actual performance and outcomes against your hypothesis to establish whether or not your assumptions and expectations were proven accurate or not. Whether you were proven right or wrong, consider the reason for the result. Was the experiment a success? And remember you can be proven wrong and still have a successful experiment. If you think moving the 'buy now' button on your website will increase sales and it doesn't, well at least you know something you didn't know before and you don't have to consider that option again. Success in any experiment is a conclusive result one way or the other.

When you are assessing results look out for any unintended consequences that occurred as a result of the experiment that you did not expect. Consider how you could better manage them if you roll out the results or how you could take advantage of them for even greater reward.

Plus consider what you've learned about the process of experimentation that you can apply for better results in the future.

Some experiments will be clear-cut and the result will point to one course of action over another. In those cases you can move forward with the implementation of the best idea as soon as possible. In other instances you may need to conduct additional follow-up tests before knowing for sure which option to pursue. For example, if the first product modification doesn't yield any difference to sales then you would need to test the control product against the second product modification and so on across all intended modifications so as to identify the one that makes the biggest positive impact on sales.

Practical example

Say you are the fundraising manager for a large environmental charity. You know direct marketing is a great way to raise funds and you have a 'control' campaign that works extremely well, but you want to see if you can lift response because direct mail can be very expensive and you want to ensure you get the most bang for your buck. So you decide to test a few different approaches to see if any alteration can cost-effectively increase results.

You have three hypotheses that you want to test:

1 'Handwritten sticky notes with a personal "ask" attached to the letter increase response'
2 'Pre-paid return envelopes increase response'
3 'Changing the order of the "ask" so that a high donation is asked for first will increase the gift size on the response form'.

To run the experiment four randomly selected files of 2,000 customers are selected from the customer universe of 500,000 active customers. One group of 2,000 customers received the control pack which is currently working well. One group of 2,000 customers gets exactly the same pack except there is a handwritten post-it note on the letter; another group of 2,000 customers receives the control pack with a pre-paid return envelope included; and the last group of 2,000 customers receives the control pack with a change to the size of initial donation request on the donation response form. Whereas the control pack provides four tick-box options starting with £20, going down to £5 with a box for 'Other', the test pack starts at £50.

All the test mailers are sent their pack on the same day so the only difference between each test is the specific issue you want to test for.

After three weeks you check on the results and find that the post-it note increased response rate the most; adding the pre-paid return envelope did not increase response at all; and the average gift size increased dramatically when you changed the order of the 'ask' on the response form. This information is of course very useful.

While the handwritten personalise ask on a post-it note increased response significantly it also increased the cost of the mailer significantly, resulting in a slight net loss. So this was shelved as a useful idea to be used for high donors only, where the additional expense would be worth it. The lack of difference in response by excluding a return envelope meant there was no need to include it, thereby making the mailer less expensive to produce. And finally the increased initial ask was implemented across the roll out which resulted in significantly more money raised.

Using business experimentation allows you to test things without the expense or risk.

Tips and traps

For business experiments to be useful you can only test one thing at a time and you must compare like with like. Seek to ensure that everything about your test is the same bar the one element you are seeking to test. For example, in the scenario above if the fundraising packs were sent on different days then that could influence the result and you might assume it was the test element and so roll out the wrong change.

Marketing tests are much easier to facilitate than product development or design tests. If you want to test prototypes then they must be of the highest quality otherwise it will skew the results. And this takes time and money.

Further reading and references

See for example:

- Anderson, E.T. and Simester, D. (2011) 'Step-by-Step Guide to Smart Business Experiments', *Harvard Business Review*, March (http://hbr .org/2011/03/a-step-by-step-guide-to-smart-business-experiments/ar/1)
- Davenport, T.H. (2009) 'How to Design Smart Business Experiments', *Harvard Business Review*, February (http://hbr.org/2009/02/ how-to-design-smart-business-experiments/ar/1)
- http://www.mindtools.com/pages/article/business-experiments.htm

2 Visual analytics

What is it?

Data can be analysed in different ways and the most simple method is to create a visual or graph and look at it to spot patterns. This is called visual analytics and is an integrated approach that combines data analysis with data visualisation and human interaction.

Data is produced at an alarming rate. In 1981 futurist and inventor Buckminster Fuller proposed the 'knowledge doubling curve' to explain the fact that the more knowledge we accumulate the faster we create more knowledge. Up until the end of the nineteenth century human knowledge doubled every one hundred years or so. By the end of the Second World War the total knowledge of mankind was doubling every 25 years. Today it is thought to be every 13 months and IBM have already predicted a point where our knowledge will double every 11 hours.

Now that's a lot of data! Unfortunately our ability to collect and store that data is increasing faster than our ability to analyse it. And while there have been a number of tools developed to automatically analyse some of it, the complexity of the data and the questions being asked means that human beings still need to be involved to bring their creativity, flexibility and background knowledge of the situation to the process. Visual analytics therefore allows decision makers to combine human input with the enormous storage and processing capacities of modern technology to gain insight into complex problems using advanced visual interfaces to help them to make better decisions.

When do I use it?

The most appropriate time to use visual analytics is when you are trying to make sense of a huge volume of data and/or if the complexity of the problem you face could be assisted by some additional computational horsepower.

Visual analytics is therefore a useful tool when you need to attack large, complex and interrelated problems where there is a lot of data to analyse. Technology is clearly essential to analytics but technology will probably never replace human beings because it's not yet possible for technology to get a 'big picture' grasp of the problem and what needs to be done from multiple different angles. Visual analytics seeks to take the best of human intellect and technology to combine them in a way that allows the technology to do most of the hard computational work while ensuring that it is solving the right problems and the end result is palatable and useful for the human being that will have to interpret it.

Technology can therefore amplify human cognitive ability by increasing cognitive resources, expanding working memory, reducing search time and enhancing pattern recognition capabilities across large data sets.

Using visual analytics when turning data into pictures and graphics would help tell a more complete story and help to reveal the patterns and trends hidden within that data, which could in turn aid decision making at all levels of your business.

What business questions is it helping me to answer?

Essentially, visual analytics can help you spot patterns in data and allow you to make vast amounts of data accessible and understandable to anyone regardless of whether they are a data scientist or statistician or not. It can help you to answer:

- Where are my best customers located?
- What is the profile of my best customers?
- Is my market share increasing or decreasing?
- Is there any connection between factor X and factor Y?

Visual analytics also allows you to answer these questions faster and provide the answers in a visual, more engaging way.

How do I use it?

According to the European project VisMaster, there are four separate stages in the visual analytics process – data, visualisation, knowledge and models. The first stage is the input and transformation of the data. Often the source data exists in different formats and in different locations so it first needs to be integrated before visual or automatic analysis methodologies can be applied. Other typical pre-processing tasks include data cleaning, normalisation and grouping.

The next step is to run the automatic analysis, which will often use data mining methods to generate models of the original data. Once a model is created you must then evaluate and refine the models. Visualisations then allow you to interact with the automatic analysis and play around with the data by modifying parameters or selecting other analysis algorithms. Model visualisation can then be used to evaluate the findings of the generated models. Alternating between visual and automatic methods is characteristic for the visual analytics process and leads to a continuous refinement and verification of preliminary findings. Remember, it is the combination of human and technology that makes visual analytics so useful. If something doesn't look right to the human eye then it can be checked, refined or new analysis run.

Ultimately it is the user interaction with the visualisation of the data that is needed to reveal insightful information, for instance by zooming in on different data areas or by considering different visual perspectives. Essentially, knowledge can be gained from visualisation, automatic analysis, as well as the preceding interactions between visualisations, models and the human being doing the analysis. Thankfully there are many commercially available visual analytics tools on the market.

Practical example

Swedish medical doctor and academic Hans Rosling is Professor of International Health at Karolinska Institute. He is also a statistician, data guru and brilliant public speaker. If you want to see the power of visual analytics then I recommend you watch any of his really interesting, funny and engaging Technology, Entertainment, Design (TED) talks.

In one (http://www.ted.com/talks/hans_rosling_at_state), he talks about how his students often discuss 'them' and 'us' in terms of the developed world and the western world or developing world. So he asked them to define exactly what they meant by these labels. They had all learned about them in college and were confident they knew what they meant. Dr Rosling pushed for a specific definition, and one student suggested that the developed world was characterised by 'long life and small families' and the developing world was characterised by 'short life and large families'. It was a neat and concise definition but was it true? Dr Rosling decided to test the hypothesis. Obviously in order to test such a theory an enormous amount of data was required to process.

He needed mortality rates per country, birth rates per country and all that data every year for decades. To look at that data in its raw form – perhaps in spreadsheets or databases – would have yielded very little in terms of insights. The human brain would not have been able to process such massive data sets and come up with any meaningful conclusions – and yet Dr Rosling did using visual analytics.

He found that the notion that his students held about the nature of life in different parts of the world was fundamentally flawed. He created a visual map that showed the correlation between 'children per woman' versus 'life expectancy' for countries across the globe and animated the chart to move through the years. Watching the visual animation of the data, viewers could tell that initially looking at data from 1950 the definition was largely accurate but by 2007 it simply wasn't true any more. And yet here were young students being taught this definition as though it was still a hard, fast and accurate definition.

Granted there were still countries such as Afghanistan where that definition still held true but the vast majority of countries had significantly reduced family numbers and were living much longer than their grandparents.

That is the power of visual analytics: it allows mind-boggling data sets to become genuinely useful and can help us to change out mindset about what is really happening in our business.

Tips and traps

When creating the visual analytics make sure that the key strategic question the data is answering is stated clearly on the page or screen. This will help to focus the reader's attention on the data's purpose so they don't get lost in the graphic or visual representation.

The key danger with visual analytics is that you can end up becoming obsessed with the visual part of the equation and slice and dice the data a thousand ways. Visual analytics is extremely useful for bridging the gap between the data and the insights but only when you stick to what's needed when it's needed. Just because a visual analytics program can present and manipulate the data a thousand different ways doesn't mean you need to present and manipulate the data a thousand different ways. Stay focused on what needs to be answered.

Further reading and references

For more on visual analytics see for example:

- Tufte, E. (2001) *The Visual Display of Quantitative Information*, 2nd edition, Cheshire, CT
- http://www.visual-analytics.eu
- http://www.sas.com/visual-analytics

3 Correlation analysis

What is it?

Correlation analysis is a statistical technique that allows you to determine whether there is a relationship between two separate variables and how strong that relationship may be.

This type of analysis is only appropriate if the data is quantified and represented by a number. It can't be used for categorical data, such as gender, brands purchased, or colour.

The analysis produces a single number between +1 and −1 that describes the degree of relationship between two variables. If the result is positive then the two variables are positively correlated to each other, i.e. when one is high, the other one tends to be high too. If the result is negative then the two variables are negatively correlated to each other, i.e. when one is high, the other one tends to be low.

So, for example, if (as a hypothetical example) correlation analysis discovered that there was a correlation of +0.73 between height and IQ then the taller someone was the higher the likelihood is that they also have a higher IQ. Conversely, if that correlation was discovered to be −0.64 then the taller someone was the more likely he or she was also to have a low IQ.

A positive score denotes direct correlation whereas a negative score denotes inverse correlation. And zero means there is no correlation between the two variables. The closer the score is towards 1 – either positive or negative – the stronger the correlation is. The result is considered 'statistically significant', i.e. important enough to pay attention to if the result is 0.5 or above in either direction.

When do I use it?

Correlation analysis is most useful when you 'know' or suspect that there is a relationship between two variables and you would like to test your assumption or hypothesis. For example, you may believe that temperature is affecting sales.

An ice-cream seller will definitely sell more ice cream in hot weather but is there a correlation between your product and service and temperature? Correlation analysis would allow you to work that out.

Alternatively you can use correlation analysis when you want to know which of several pairs of variable shows the strongest correlation. So you may want to see whether temperature affects sales more than time of year for example.

And finally you can use this type of analysis speculatively on quantifiable data sets to see what emerges. Sometimes correlation analysis will highlight an unexpected relationship that could warrant further analysis and potential exploitation. For example, Walmart discovered an unexpected relationship between the purchase of Pop-Tarts and a hurricane warning. Apparently when there was a severe weather warning in the US, the sale of Pop-Tarts increased. This knowledge allowed Walmart to position Pop-Tarts at the entrance of the store following a hurricane warning, further pushing up sales. An unexpected correlation was also discovered between beer sales and nappy sales in the United States. Presumably the father sent to buy nappies would be reminded that he wouldn't be going out this weekend and bought some beer instead. These types of insights can of course be extremely useful and lead to even higher sales with a little in-store product positioning.

What business questions is it helping me to answer?

Essentially, correlation analysis can help you to make connections between quantifiable variables that can help you to make better decisions and improve performance. It can help you to answer:

- Are our most loyal customers also our most profitable?
- Do customers purchase more when the price is lower?
- Does pay influence length of tenure?
- Does number of annual holidays influence absenteeism?
- Is there any relationship between factor X and factor Y?

Correlation analysis can be essential for testing assumptions prior to alterations in strategy or product mix.

How do I use it?

If you are feeling brave and you have a scientific calculator to hand then you can use what is known as 'Pearson's correlation coefficient'[®].

$$r = \frac{\sum XY - \frac{(\sum X)(\sum Y)}{n}}{\sqrt{\left(\sum X^2 - \frac{(\sum X)^2}{n}\right)\left(\sum Y^2 - \frac{(\sum Y)^2}{n}\right)}}$$

1   First you need to gather your data for the two variables you want to analyse. You can calculate the correlation for any quantifiable data set.

2   Create a spreadsheet or table that lists the data sets vertically in columns. In the first column, labelled x, add all the data for your first variable (x) and in the second column, labelled y, add all the data for your second variable (y).

3   Label column three, four and five 'x y', 'x x' and 'y y' respectively.

4   Perform the relevant calculations in column three, four and five, i.e. 'x y' = x multiplied by y, 'x x' = x multiplied by x, and 'y y' = y multiplied by y.

5   Add all the values in each column and add the total at the bottom of each column.

6   Insert the numbers into the equation to establish the correlation between the variables under investigation.

Alternatively you can use software and there are many correlation tools on the market.
    You can make your life a little easier by using desktop software such as Microsoft Excel that contains pre-installed formulas to calculate your correlations. There are many simple online tutorials available to explain how you use it.

Practical example

Say you wanted to find out whether there was a relationship between the price you charged for your product and the number of units sold at that price. Often the assumption is that the cheaper a product is the more units of that product you are likely to sell, but that hypothesis does not always hold true. Considering how important price and sales are to revenue and growth you decide it's time to actually establish if that assumption is true or not.

x (price)	y (units sold)	x y	x x	y y
5.00	56	280	25	3136
7.50	54	405	56.25	2916
10.00	50	500	100	2500
15.00	40	600	225	1600
	37.5	1785	406.25	10152

$\Sigma xy = (5)(56) + (7.50)(54) + (10)(50) + (15)(40) = 1785$

$\Sigma x = 5 + 7.50 + 10 + 15 = 37.5$

$\Sigma y = 56 + 54 + 50 + 40 = 200$

$\Sigma x^2 = 25 + 56.25 + 100 + 225 = 406.25$

$\Sigma y^2 = 3136 + 2916 + 2500 + 1600 = 10152$

$$r = \frac{\Sigma XY - \frac{(\Sigma X)(\Sigma Y)}{n}}{\sqrt{\left(\Sigma X^2 - \frac{(\Sigma X)^2}{n}\right)\left(\Sigma Y^2 - \frac{(\Sigma Y)^2}{n}\right)}}$$

So:

$$R = \frac{1785 - \frac{(37.5)(200)}{4}}{\sqrt{\left(406.25 - \frac{(37.5)^2}{4}\right)\left(10152 - \frac{(200)^2}{4}\right)}} = -0.389$$

This result indicates that there is no statistically significant correlation between price and unit sold.

Tips and traps

If you already have the data, you might like to try some speculative correlation analysis to see if you can find unexpected relationships or connections that you could exploit for additional sales.

If two variables are correlated that does not imply that one caused the other it simply means there is a relationships between them. Don't be caught out by assuming causation. Equally, just because two variables are not correlated does not mean they are independent of each other.

Remember, establishing a correlation between two variables is not a sufficient condition to state categorically that there is a causal relationship between the two. A business experiment would help to clarify if a causal relationship does exist.

Further reading and references

Correlation analysis is a basic statistical method that is covered in more detail in most statistics books and websites. See for example:

- Urdan, T. (2010) *Good Books are Statistics in Plain English*, London: Routledge
- Rumsey, D. (2011) *Statistics For Dummies*, Hoboken, NJ: Wiley Publishing

4   Scenario analysis

What is it?

Scenario analysis, also known as horizon analysis or total return analysis, is a method of projection. It is an analytic process that allows you to analyse a variety of possible future events or 'scenarios' by considering alternative possible outcomes.

By planning out the detail required to implement a particular decision or course of action you can observe not only the final potential outcome but also the viability of the path leading to that outcome. Often it's only when you really consider what would be involved in the actual implementation of an idea that you fully appreciate the scope of that idea. Scenario analysis therefore allows you to improve decision making by fully considering the outcomes you expect and their implementation implications without the cost and time involved in actual real-world implementation.

Scenario analysis does not rely on historical data and doesn't expect the future to be the same as the past or seek to extrapolate the past into the future, rather it tries to consider possible future developments and turning points.

When do I use it?

Use scenario analysis when you are unsure which decision to take or which course of action to pursue. It can be especially useful if the implications of the decision are significant. For example, if the decision would cost a great deal of time or money to implement or if the ramifications of getting the decision wrong could be fatal for the business then scenario analysis can be a very powerful tool.

It can be used to assess the possible likely future of different strategic choices or it can be used to generate a combination of different scenarios that look at the same scenario but from three different perspectives – the optimistic version of events, the pessimistic version of events and the most likely scenario.

It is also a very useful tool if you are unclear about what is going to be involved in the execution of a strategy or decision as the process required pushes you to really engage with the scenario you are testing. This amplified engagement can help to anticipate more of the pros and cons of each scenario therefore reducing risk and directing you to the best choice.

What business questions is it helping me to answer?

Scenario analysis can help the decision-making process by looking at the likely implications of that decision and how it might or could pan out in the future. It can help you to answer:

- Which strategic direction do we take?
- What are the best countries to expand our business into?
- Do I open in a new location or upgrade or expand the retail stores I currently have?
- Do I invest in a new market or seek to increase market share in the one I'm already in?

Scenario analysis can help to prevent errors of judgement and direct strategy.

How do I use it?

Essentially, what you are doing in scenario analysis is attempting to work out if the world would turn out a certain way if certain conditions were met. The process usually consists of a five-stage process:

1 Define the problem.
2 Gather the data.
3 Separate certainties from uncertainties.
4 Develop scenarios.
5 Use the outcome in your planning.

Define the problem

Obviously the only reason you would use scenario analysis is if you were trying to gain insight into a particular challenge. The first step is therefore to define the problem you are trying to solve or gain greater understanding of it so that you can make the best decision.

It is also important to think about the time horizon. Most decisions need to be made within a timeline so make sure you have enough time to conduct the scenario analysis before the decision needs to be made.

Gather the data

So what is going to affect or influence the scenario you are considering? Identify what data and information you need to make the analysis as realistic as possible.

You may, for example, consider trends and what uncertainties exist around your scenario.

You could use PESTLE analysis as a guide in gathering data – what could affect the outcome when you consider politics, economy, social, technical, legal and environmental issues? Also seek to identify the key assumptions on which the plan might depend.

Separate the certainties from the uncertainties

You will invariably come into the analysis process with a host of assumptions and preconceptions about how the analysis will turn out. It is important that you become aware of what those assumptions are so you can really shine a light of enquiry on to those assumptions and separate the certainties from the uncertainties.

Take a moment to challenge all your current assumptions and decide if they are certainties or uncertainties. It is always best to err on the side of caution; that way if the outcome is better than expected it's a bonus, whereas an outcome worse than expected could be a disaster and would negate the whole purpose of running the analysis in the first place.

List the uncertainties in order of priority with the largest, most significant uncertainties at the top.

Develop scenarios

Starting with the top uncertainty – what would you consider to be a good outcome for that uncertainty? What would be a bad outcome? Once you've done this develop a story of the future around each that marries the certainties with the outcome you've chosen.

Do the same with each of the major uncertainties you've listed.

Use the scenarios in your planning

This process will give you much more knowledge and clarity around the situation you face and you can use the scenarios to influence and guide your planning.

There are commercially available scenario analysis tools on the market that can make scenario planning much easier.

Practical example

Scenario analysis is essentially a planning tool that can allow you to identify various factors that could affect a proposed plan and assess how those factors may play out in the future so you can see which alternative is most likely to work out well.

Say you are planning to start a new business that helps clients implement a specific new software program. You want the business to be turning over £1 million within five years. But is that feasible? A friend suggests that you run some scenario analysis to help you get a clear picture of that challenge and how likely that outcome really is.

You gather data on trends and current realities. Among other things, you discover that people tend to hold off on buying new hardware and software during a recession and you are currently in a recession. That said, economic pressure also increases potential customers' desire to increase productivity and your software can meet that need. The software vendor is also working on an upgrade that is already at beta testing, so your clients could potentially reap even greater rewards. The only possible challenge is that your software is quite new and innovative so you are unsure how quickly you could recruit consultants to implement the software.

Next stage is to separate certainties from uncertainties. The current economy is an uncertainty, but the recession has definitely increased the number of people looking for work so you can feel more confident that you can find the necessary employees to make this work. You realise you haven't actually seen the beta version of the upgrade so you visit the vendor to see what's in the pipeline and are certain that the new version will be even more beneficial to your clients. What is uncertain, however, is whether or not any other software company is working on anything similar or better that could seriously undermine your planning and potential outcome.

Based on what you've discovered you create three scenarios to test:

- Best-case scenario assumes that the economy pulls out of recession and grows steadily over the next five years. It also assumes that you've chosen the right software and that no big company swoops in and surpasses your software.

- No great scenario assumes the recession continues for at least another two years, which would probably mean that at least 25 per cent of your clients would choose to defer their investment.

- Worst-case scenario assumes that a global software giant does enter your market and establishes itself within two years. This would definitely put pressure on your new business.

Having looked at the scenarios and considered their planning implications you realise that most of the risk is in the short term. While the economy is a challenge, you could take advantage of this by educating clients in the productivity improvements that software will deliver. The bigger issue is the possibility of another player entering the market with better software, so you decide to make the business flexible by hiring a mix of full-time and contract workers so you can scale up and scale down quickly depending on what actually happens. Plus you need to keep a very keen eye on what rival software companies are doing so you can cross-train personnel if necessary.

By appreciating the very real threat a rival software company poses to your business you can anticipate that challenge, and are well positioned to monitor it closely so that it does not have the chance to de-rail your plans.

Tips and traps

While the outcome of scenario analysis can greatly facilitate better decision making and help to reduce the risk of big decisions, the process of the analysis is probably more important. By creating a few scenarios – even the out of left-field scenario – you can end up uncovering new information or insights that were previously unknown that can not only assist the outcome but what's happening in the business right now.

That said, it's easy to assume that what you think you know about the current situation is true and jump to conclusions, or automatically assume that you are certain about some of the influencing factors. Scenario analysis will always yield the best results when you challenge all your assumptions in the process.

Further reading and references

A lot of the information in this section is based on the great information provided on the Mind Tools website:

- http://www.mindtools.com/pages/article/newSTR_98.htm

Other useful sites include:

- http://www.wisegeek.com/what-is-scenario-analysis.htm
- http://www.scenarioanalysis.net/

Forecasting/time series analysis

What is it?

To understand what time series analysis is you must first understand what time series data is. Essentially, time series data is data that is collected at uniformly spaced intervals. For example, the closing value of the FTSE is time series data, or the annual flow volume of the Thames is time series data because the data is measured consistently at particular times to plot the changes.

Time series analysis explores this data to extract meaningful statistics or data characteristics. The data collected is not random but rather it is based on the assumption that successive values in the data file represent consecutive measurements taken at equally spaced time intervals.

Time series analysis is a forecasting methodology that seeks to forecast what will happen in the future based on what did happen in the past. By analysing time series data the idea is that you will be able to identify patterns that can then be extrapolated into the future.

When do I use it?

You would use time series analysis when you want to identify the nature of the phenomenon represented by the sequence of data observations in order to assess changes over time. Or it can be used when you want to forecast the observable phenomenon into the future.

Both of these goals require that the pattern of observed time series data is identified and formally described. Once the pattern is established, we can interpret and integrate it with other data such as weather, season or sales figures to come up with a theory that can then be tested.

Time series data is usually plotted via a line chart and this type of analysis is frequently used in statistics, pattern recognition, mathematics and finance, and in weather forecasting such as severe weather or earthquake prediction.

What business questions is it helping me to answer?

Time series analysis can help the decision making to predict the future. It can help you to answer:

- What will be the economic performance of a business, region, country over the next months?
- To what extent will I be able to improve my production process for this product over the next months?
- What will be the demand for jobs in our sector over the coming years?

How do I use it?

You need to gather time series data and seek to remove any errors. Most time series analysis techniques involve some form of filtering out errors, often known as noise, in order to make the pattern more noticeable.

The identified patterns can be described either as a trend or seasonality. Essentially a trend represents a general systematic pattern that changes over time but does not repeat within the time range. Seasonality may have a similar nature over time but it will repeat itself in systematic intervals.

Both may coexist in real-life data. For example, sales may grow steadily over time and also spike consistently around Christmas.

Two of the most common processes for conducting time series analysis are:

- autoregressive process;
- moving average process.

The equations for these calculations are not for the faint-hearted but if you would like to know more, refer to the references and further reading section at the end of this chapter. Alternatively there are many commercially available time series analysis tools on the market.

Practical example

Perhaps you've been asked to provide quarterly forecasts of sales for one of your products over the coming year. These forecasts are important because they will influence production schedules, the purchase of raw materials, inventory and ware-housing policies, and sales quotas. If you get the forecast wrong then too many or too few products could be made, which would affect the sales department and warehousing not to mention what could happen to your brand and reputation with your customers.

You could rely on good judgement, cross your fingers or hope for the best, or you could conduct some time series analysis to identify trends or changes to sales based on seasonality so that you can more accurately predict sales in the coming year.

Because you have historical quantitative data about the variable being forecast, and it is reasonable to assume that nothing out of the ordinary is going to happen in the coming year and that therefore the past results will provide a useful projection into the future, then time series analysis can certainly help to reduce the risk.

Tips and traps

Time series analysis can be a quick and insightful way to identify trends in results but its accuracy comes down to the quality of the data and an appreciation of 'other' factors that could be influencing the trend.

For time series analysis to be genuinely useful you will need to be very confident in the accuracy and reliability of the historical data the analysis is based on. Plus it is easy to mistake cyclical trends for long-term influences. You may, for example, assume a dip in sales over a few months is some sort of cyclical glitch when it could in fact be due to the impact of a new competitor. By making the assumption that it is a glitch you could forecast too high. If your market or business is going through a period of change then forecasting the future based on the past is probably not going to be the best forecasting technique.

Further reading and references

Time series analysis is an advanced statistical method that is covered in more detail in most advanced statistics books and websites. See for example:

- www.statsoft.com/Textbook/Time-Series-Analysis
- http://itfeature.com/time-series-analysis-and-forecasting/time-series-analysis-forecasting
- www.cengage.com/resource_uploads/downloads/113318765X_342117.pdf

6　Data mining

What is it?

Data mining is often used as a buzzword of generic description applied to any form of large-scale information processing, but this is not very accurate. Plus the term itself is actually a misnomer because it implies that the goal is the data extraction rather than the insights that data can yield.

More accurately, data mining is an analytic process designed to explore data, usually very large business-related data sets – also known as 'big data' – in search for commercially relevant insights, patterns or relationships between variables that can improve results and elevate performance.

Data mining is essentially a hybrid of artificial intelligence, statistics, database systems, database research and machine learning. And the actual process is the automatic or semi-automatic analysis of large data sets to extract previously unknown yet interesting patterns, anomalies or dependencies that could be exploited.

When do I use it?

The ultimate goal of data mining is prediction, so you would use data mining if you had large data sets and wanted to extract insights from that data that could help your business in the future.

Clearly in business, being able to predict the future is helpful and can not only reduce costs and assist with planning and strategy, but insights gained from data mining could potentially change the direction of the business.

Insights extracted from data mining can also guide decision making and reduce risk. It is important to appreciate, however, that data mining may throw up patterns, anomalies or inter-dependencies, but it will not necessarily tell you the reason for those patterns, anomalies or inter-dependencies. Additional analysis will be required if the 'why' is still important to you.

What business questions is it helping me to answer?

Data mining can help the decision maker to predict the future. It can help you to answer:

- What are the key factors that our most profitable customers have in common?
- How could we categorise our customers in the smart watch segment?
- What factors are common in fraudulent transactions?
- What are the key patterns people use to navigate our website?

How do I use it?

There are three stages in data mining:

- the initial exploration;
- model building and validation;
- deployment.

Stage 1: Initial exploration

First you need to prepare the data, which involves cleaning the data, data transformations, selecting data subsets. Plus if the data sets are large and have large numbers of variable fields then some sort of preliminary feature selection will be required to bring the variables to a manageable range.

Then, depending on the nature of the analytic problem, initial exploration may involve a simple choice of straightforward predictors for a regression model all the way to elaborate exploratory analyses in order to identify the most relevant variables and determine the complexity and the general nature of the models that can be taken into account in the next stage.

Stage 2: Model building and validation

Next you need to consider the various models you've identified in stage one so you can choose the best one based on their predictive performance. This may sound like a simple operation, but in fact it sometimes involves a very elaborate process. There are a variety of techniques developed to achieve that goal – many of which are based on so-called 'competitive evaluation of models', i.e. applying different models to the same data set and then comparing their performance to choose the best.

Core techniques of predictive data mining that are the most popular include: Bagging, Boosting, Stacking and Meta-Learning. For more information on these see the 'Statsoft' website link at the end of this chapter.

The final stage of data mining involves using the model selected as being the best from the previous stage and applying it to new data in order to generate predictions or estimates of the expected outcome.

The best way to capitalise on data mining is to invest in one of the many data mining tools on the market.

Practical example

Data mining can throw up unusual and unexpected connections between variables that can then be exploited to increase results. As seen earlier in Chapter 3, using data mining Walmart discovered that the sale of Pop-Tarts increased whenever there was a hurricane warning.

Increased sales in flashlights may have been expected but why people suddenly felt the urge to stock up on sugary breakfast treats was not. But Walmart didn't need to know 'why' there was a connection only that there was a connection.

By positioning the Pop-Tarts display at the front of the store whenever there was a hurricane or severe weather warning Walmart were then able to boost sales still further.

Tips and traps

More and more people are more and more concerned about the data that is held on them inside big business and what those businesses are doing with it. These concerns are only going to grow so always use data ethically and transparently. Tell your customers what you want to do with their data and make sure that the outcome delivers value to them as well as your business.

Consider anonymising the data so that the information is not traceable to a particular person. Often the insights are not customer specific. For example, Walmart didn't need to know who bought Pop-Tarts in a hurricane they just needed to identify the trend to capitalise on it.

Never underestimate the value of the data you hold or your obligation to protect it. Data is the new currency and you need to protect the privacy of your customers internally and externally.

Further reading and references

Data mining is an advanced analytics method that is covered in more detail in many advanced statistics books and websites. See for example:

- Brown, M. S. (2014) *Data Mining For Dummies*, Hoboken, NJ: John Wiley & Sons; 1st edition

- Witten, I.H., Frank, E. and Hall, M.A. (2011) *Data Mining: Practical Machine Learning Tools and Techniques*, 3rd edition, Burlington, MA: Morgan Kaufmann Publishers
- http://www.statsoft.com/textbook/data-mining-techniques
- http://www.anderson.ucla.edu/faculty/jason.frand/teacher/technologies/palace/datamining.htm
- http://www.sas.com/en_us/insights/analytics/data-mining.html

7

Regression analysis

What is it?

Regression analysis is a statistical tool for investigating the relationship between variables. For instance, is there a causal relationship between price and product demand?

Regression analysis is often talked about alongside correlation analysis and as such it's often quite difficult to know which is which and what the difference is. Essentially, regression analysis identifies the relationships between two variables and plots the course of that relationship which can then be predicted into the future, whereas correlation analysis explores the strength of that relationship.

Regression analysis is a mainstay of economics but has become an increasingly important technique in other fields such as law and government policy. The findings of regression analysis have, for example, been offered as evidence of liability, evidence of racial bias and evidence of voting violations in legal cases.

When do I use it?

You could use regression analysis if you believe that one variable is affecting another and you want to establish whether your hypothesis is true. In order to do so you need to assemble data on the underlying variables you are interested in so that you can employ regression analysis to estimate the quantitative effect of the causal variables upon the variable that they influence.

You can also gauge the 'statistical significance' of the estimated relationships. In other words how confident you can be that there is a close and therefore predictable relationship between the variables.

What business questions is it helping me to answer?

Regression analysis can help the decision maker to identify relationships and help predict the future. It can help you to answer:

- Is customer loyalty or customer satisfaction driving profitability?
- Is our brand image and reputation leading to increased sales?
- Is the quality of our products leading to increased customer satisfaction?
- Are engaged employees more loyal?

How do I use it?

At the start of any regression analysis you need to formulate a hypothesis about the relationship between the variables of interest. You may, for example, believe that the more educated someone is the more money they will earn. The tentative hypothesis for this assertion could be 'higher levels of educational attainment cause higher levels of earnings where all other things are equal'.

You would then need to test this hypothesis using a regression model. Regression models involve the following variables:

- the unknown parameters, denoted as β;
- the independent variables, X;
- the dependent variable, Y.

A regression model relates Y to a function of X and β.

$$Y \approx f(X, \beta)$$

Obviously it gets considerably more complex than the above equation. The general computational problem that needs to be solved in regression analysis is to fit a straight line to a number of variable and non-variable points usually visualised in a scatterplot diagram. This can be done via a number of approaches including:

- least squares;
- the regression equation;
- unique prediction and partial correlation;
- predicted and residual scores;
- residual variance and R-square;
- interpreting the correlation coefficient R.

If you want to know more about these explore the links at the end of the chapter. Alternatively there are many commercially available regression analysis tools on the market that can help you.

You can make your life a little easier by using desktop software such as Microsoft Excel that contains preinstalled formulas to calculate your regressions. There are many simple online tutorials available to explain how you use it.

Practical example

An estate agent might use regression analysis to understand more about his market and increase sales and revenue.

For example, the agent might collect data for all his listings including the size of the house in square metres, number of bedrooms, number of reception rooms, average income in the respective area according to census data, how long the property was on the market and any subjective rating about the appeal of the house.

He could then use regression analysis to measure whether and how these variables relate to the price the house is then sold for. He might, for example, learn that the number of bedrooms was a better price predictor than how long the property was listed for. Or that the square metreage predicted price far better than whether the subjective measure suggested the home was attractive or not.

The agent may also be able to use regression to find anomalies and price those properties higher because he understands the market in more depth.

Tips and traps

The advantage of regression analysis is that it's a familiar technique and it is powerful and flexible. But familiarity can breed contempt, so you need to check the validity of your source data and really question the assumptions that you hold around your hypothesis. For example, you could assume that the higher the education the higher the salary, but there are a multitude of other causal factors that could distort your findings.

The biggest traps regarding regression analysis are the assumptions you make and the quality of the data you use. Check both.

Further reading and references

Regression analysis is a basic statistical method that is covered in more detail in most statistics books and websites. See for example:

- Urdan, T. (2010) *Good Books are Statistics in Plain English*, London: Routledge
- Rumsey, D. (2011) *Statistics For Dummies*, Hoboken, NJ: Wiley Publishing
- http://www.law.uchicago.edu/files/files/20.Sykes_.Regression.pdf
- http://www.statsoft.com/Textbook/Multiple-Regression
- http://people.duke.edu/~rnau/regex.htm

Text analytics

8

What is it?

Text analytics, also known as text mining, is a process of extracting value from large quantities of unstructured text data.

Most businesses have a huge amount of text-based data from memos, company documents, emails, reports, media releases, customer records and communication, websites, blogs and social media posts. Until recently, however, it wasn't always that useful. While the text is structured to make sense to a human being it is unstructured from an analytics perspective because it doesn't fit neatly into a relational database or rows and columns of a spreadsheet.

The only structured part of text traditionally was the name of the document, the date it was created and who created it – all of which could be searched for easier retrieval at a later date. Plus of course you can search a document to find a particular word or phrase, but this type of enquiry requires us to know already what we are looking for.

Text analytics is now capable of telling us things we didn't already know and, perhaps more importantly, had no way of knowing before. Access to huge text data sets and improved technical capability means text can be analysed to extract additional high-quality information above and beyond what the document actually says. For example, text can be assessed for commercially relevant patterns such as an increase or decrease in positive feedback from customers, new insights that could lead to product tweaking or other interesting anomaly. And these insights can be incredibly useful in business.

When do I use it?

There are a number of reasons why you might use text analytics. Essentially, there are five main text analytics tasks:

- text categorisation;
- text clustering;

- concept extraction;
- sentiment analysis;
- document summarisation.

Text analytics assigns a document to one or more classes or categories according to the subject or according to other attributes such as document type, author, creation date, etc. Text categorisation applies some structure to the text which can then be used for analysis or query. This can be helpful if you have a huge amount of text data that needs to be classified for easier access and usability.

Spam filters use text classification to assess the text within incoming emails and decide if the email is legitimate or not. Email routing also uses this technique to re-route an email arriving at a general address to a more appropriate recipient based on the topic discussed in the text of the email.

Text clustering allows you to automatically cluster huge amounts of text into meaningful topics or categories for fast information retrieval or filtering.

Search engines use text clustering to deliver meaningful search results. For example, if you enter 'cell' into a search engine the results would be clustered around 'biology', 'battery' and 'prison' – all of which use a different definition of the word 'cell'.

Concept extraction is particularly useful if you have a great deal of data that you need to access but need to do quickly to deliver results. These techniques are used in law firms, for example, where there are literally millions of past case documents from their own and other legal cases. Concept extraction analytics can hone in on the documents that are likely to be most relevant to the new case, thus saving expensive personnel a huge amount of time trying to locate documents to use in court.

Sentiment analysis is particularly useful if you want to discover trends, patterns and hidden consensus within text over and above what the text actually says. Sentiment analysis, also known as opinion mining, seeks to extract subjective opinion or sentiment from text so that you can extract whether the data is positive, negative or neutral.

Finally, data summarisation allows you to automatically summarise documents using a computer program to retain the most important points from the original document. This can be really useful if you have a lot of reading to get through but not enough time. Search engines also use this technology to summarise websites on result listings.

What business questions is it helping me to answer?

Text analytics is particularly useful for information retrieval, pattern recognition, tagging and annotation, information extraction, sentiment assessment and predictive analytics. In essence it's about getting more information from text and helping text to be even more useful over and above the actual meaning of the text.

As such, it can help you to answer:

- What do my customers/employees think of my product? (See sentiment analysis in Chapter 9)

- What is the perception of our employment brand among Twitter users?
- What are the most important issues customers complain to us about?
- What are key trends based on the search terms people use on our website?

How do I use it?

First, the text that you want to analyse must be datafied not just digitised. This is an important distinction.

By some estimates more than 130 million books have been published since the invention of the Gutenberg printing press in 1450. By 2012 the Google Book Project had scanned over 20 million titles or more than 15 per cent of the world's entire written heritage! That's a lot of text. If you copied a page from a book as a jpeg file or took a picture of a page in a book you would technically have a digital copy of the text but that would be of no value to you if you wanted to run text analytics.

What you need is datafied text like the text we see in many e-readers. E-readers such as the Kobo or the Amazon Kindle are not just allowing you to read a digital image of the page, you can interact with the text. You can, for example, change font size, add notes, highlight text or search for specific words and phrases in the book. For most businesses their text will already be datafied, but if you store old customer records in paper files or even microfiche then that needs to be datafied – and that doesn't' just mean taking an electronic copy of the document: it effectively means re-creating it in digital form.

It is also important to remove 'stop words' from the text being analysed. A stop word is a word like 'a', 'the', 'of', etc., which appear frequently in all text but don't communicate any unique information about the content or meaning of the text.

Once the text is ready there are a number of text analytics options open to you and which one you use will depend on your objective.

If you want to know more about the various text analytic techniques and how to use them then explore the links at the end of the chapter. Alternatively there are many commercially available text analytic tools on the market that can help you.

Practical example

You may be concerned about the level of employee engagement and decide to conduct an employee engagement survey.

The easiest way to collect this type of data is to create some form of quantitative survey that may ask employees to rate their employer and their opinion on a scale for a number of different questions. But the real nuggets of wisdom usually come from open-ended questions that allow employees to elaborate on their opinions and provide examples. But that type of qualitative data is much harder to assess. You could read through hundreds of questionnaires and that might give you some good ideas, or a sense of who is happy and who is not, but it wouldn't really give you any indication of trends or what the collective was really feeling. Text analytics would allow you to assess all that free-flowing unstructured text and establish trends or clusters of opinion in the business, divisions and within specific teams.

The surveys could, for example, be converted into a word cloud which would collate all the text data from the questionnaires and distribute that data according to how many people mentioned that word. The biggest word in a word cloud therefore refers to the word that was used by the most number of people. If the largest word on an employee engagement survey word cloud was 'resentment' or 'unhappy' then clearly you've got problems.

I know one organisation that uses text analytics to avoid having to do these types of surveys in the first place. Instead they simply scan and analyse the content of emails sent by their staff as well as the social media posts they make on Facebook or Twitter. This allows them to accurately understand the levels of staff engagement without the time and expense of a traditional survey.

Tips and traps

Just because you have text data doesn't mean you need to apply text analytics to it. Make sure you know what you are trying to discover or be otherwise clear about your objective and the reason for the analysis.

Often business owners or senior executives can get really excited about text analytics, especially when they consider the vast amount of text-based data that exists in their archive room or basement. But converting paper-based text documents into something that can be used for text analysis can be a very time-consuming and expensive process, so make sure you have a really valid reason for doing it. Besides, most data has a shelf life so if it's too old it won't help you that much anyway. Focus on the new text data you already have access to.

Further reading and references

Text analytics is usually performed using commercial software and many vendors like SAS and IBM SPSS provide very good reading material. See for example:

- www.sas.com and ww.ibm.com/textanalytics
- http://www.statsoft.com/Textbook/Text-Mining
- http://people.ischool.berkeley.edu/~hearst/papers/acl99/acl99-tdm.html
- http://libereurope.eu/wp-content/uploads/Text%20and%20Data%20Mining%20Factsheet.pdf

Sentiment analysis

9

What is it?

Sentiment analysis, also known as opinion mining, seeks to extract subjective opinion or sentiment from text (Chapter 8), video (Chapter 11) or audio data (Chapter 12).

The basic aim of sentiment analysis is to determine the attitude of an individual or group regarding a particular topic or overall context. The sentiment or attitude may be a judgement, evaluation or emotional reaction.

For example, we have known for decades that the words we use to communicate and express ourselves and our opinions only account for 7 per cent of comprehension. The vast majority of our communication is picked up non-verbally through body language and tonality. Most of us have, for example, experienced asking our children to clear the dishes, or asked an employee to stay late at work and although the words coming out of their mouth may indicate they agree – we are left in no doubt about what they really want to do!

Sentiment analysis seeks to get to the real truth behind communication so that businesses can make better decisions by working out if stakeholders feel positively, negatively or neutrally about our products, business and brand.

When do I use it?

You would use sentiment analysis when you wanted to know stakeholder opinion.

Say you have a lot of text data from your customers. That may originate from emails, surveys, social media posts, etc. There are several hundreds of thousands of words in the English language and while some are neutral, others have a distinctly positive or negative vibe. This polarity of sentiment can therefore be applied to your customer text to establish what your customers as a stakeholder group *really* think of you.

There are number of software tools that can help you to measure text sentiment around your product or service. Twitrratr, for example, allows you to separate the positive tweets about your company, brand, product or service from the negative and neutral tweets so you can see how well you are doing in the Twitterverse.

What business questions is it helping me to answer?

Sentiment analysis can help you to gauge opinion, which can in turn guide strategy and help decision making. It can help answer:

- How positive do our customers feel about our brand?
- How does the perception of our product compare to that of products from our competitors?
- What is the perception of our employment brand?

How do I use it?

Obviously what someone thinks and feels is very subjective so the data you have in order to analyse this subjective element would need to indicate sentiment in some measureable way.

This could be text, audio or video. You can, after all, tell whether someone is happy, angry, happy, excited, etc., by the words they use, the pitch and tonality of their speech, and their facial expressions.

As a result you can apply sentiment analysis to text, speech (audio) and visual interactions (video).

Advanced, 'beyond polarity' sentiment analysis can also go further by making a classification as to the emotional state involved. For example, text, audio tonality or facial expressions can determine whether the person is 'frustrated', 'angry' or 'happy'. This type of analytics is becoming increasingly popular with the rise of social media, blogs and social networks where people are sharing their thoughts and feelings about all sorts of things – including companies and products – much more readily.

It is also being used to measure emotional charge on telephone waiting queues or insurance claims lines. Tonality of voice may, for example, indicate that someone is getting upset or it may indicate that they are telling a lie!

In the current business landscape it is increasingly important that we know what our customers, competitors and employees think about the business, products and brand, and sentiment analytics can help us do that – often relatively inexpensively.

If you want to know more about the various sentiment analysis techniques and how to use them you can explore the links at the end of this chapter. Alternatively there are many commercially available sentiment analysis tools on the market that can help you.

Practical examples

Researchers at the Microsoft Research Labs in Washington discovered that it was possible to predict which women were at risk of postnatal depression just by analysing their Twitter posts with text-based sentiment analysis.

The research focused on verbal cues that the mother would use weeks before giving birth. Those who struggle with motherhood tended to use words that hinted at an underlying anxiety and unhappiness. There was more negativity in the language used with an increase in words such as 'disappointed', 'miserable', 'hate' as well as an increase in the use of 'I' – indicating a disconnection from the 'we' of impending parenthood.

Co-director of Microsoft Labs Eric Horvitz acknowledged that this type of information can be incredibly useful in reaching out and helping women at this vulnerable time and also to help break down the stigma around postnatal depression. It would be a relatively simple step, for example, for a welfare group to create an app that could run on a smartphone and alert pregnant women to the onset of potential postnatal depression and direct them to resources to help them cope.

Audio sentiment analytics is also being used to measure stress levels in call centre's so that customer service representatives can measure how upset the caller is and intervene earlier before things escalate. For example, people often talk into the receiver, even when they are on hold or listening to the soothing music; they can also make various sounds such as heavy sighing which can indicate the caller is getting increasingly frustrated.

Tips and traps

Sentiment analytics is pretty funky stuff because it can tell us things we didn't know and had no way of understanding in the past. This makes it appealing and sexy so make sure you are not just sucked in because it sounds like a useful thing to do.

Like all analytics it is only useful if there is a commercially viable reason for doing it. Make sure there is.

Further reading and references

Sentiment analytics is usually performed using commercial (and sometimes free) software and many vendors like SAS, IBM and others provide very good reading material. See for example:

- http://www.statsoft.com/Solutions/Marketing/Sentiment-Analysis
- http://www.cs.uic.edu/~liub/FBS/NLP-handbook-sentiment-analysis.pdf
- http://mashable.com/2010/04/19/sentiment-analysis/

10 Image analytics

Image analytics is the process of extracting information, meaning and insights from images such as photographs, medical images or graphics. As a process it relies heavily on pattern recognition, digital geometry and signal processing.

In the past the only analysis that was possible on images was via the human eye or if computers were used they could only really assess the name of the image or any of the meta-tags that are stored against the image such as the date of creation, amendment, the owner of the image and the name it was given. For example, if you enter 'pink elephant' into an online search engine the search engine isn't scrolling through the index to find pictures that match the description of a pink elephant, it is scrolling through the index to find meta-tags that match 'pink' and/or 'elephant'. In other words when the person who uploaded the image uploaded the image they added descriptor key words to the image to help people find it. That said, just because the tag mentions pink elephant doesn't mean that the image will relate in any way to pink elephants. As a result any analysis was basic and prone to errors.

Now image analytics is considerably more sophisticated. For example, image analytics is now being used on medical images of biopsies to help doctors identify cancer. In the case of photographs a digital photograph contains a lot more information than you might imagine; it will record when it was taken as well as where it was taken based on GPS coordinates embedded in the photo. All those additional properties can be analysed to extract more information above and beyond the actual image. Plus, one of the most exciting, and some would argue scary, developments in image analytics is face recognition.

When do I use it?

There are many applications for image analytics that could prove commercially relevant.

Face recognition analytics, for example, can automatically identify or verify a person from a digital image or video frame. This can be useful if you want to introduce an extra layer of security to your factory or premises. There could be an image of all your employees and image analytics would grant those people and only those people access to the premises. In addition, image analytics can potentially be used for marketing.

Facial recognition algorithms used to pick out facial features and analyse their relative position, size, shape, etc., or it would take a gallery of face images, normalise them and only save the distinct elements for facial recognition. These algorithms were therefore either geometric, which looks at distinguishing features, or photometric, which is a statistical approach that distils an image into values and compares the values with templates to eliminate variances. Advances in 3D face recognition technology mean that face recognition is now much more accurate.

Unsurprisingly, companies like Facebook are already ahead of the curve when it comes to face recognition because of the vast image data sets users willingly upload. Indeed Facebook researchers have reported that their DeepFace pattern recognition system is achieving near-human face recognition accuracy.

It is now possible, for example, for Facebook to recognise a face, compare it to previous photographs of that person and 'decide' if that person has put on weight. If they have, that data could then be sold to a weight loss company who would advertise on that users Facebook page.

What business questions is it helping me to answer?

Image analytics can help you secure your premises and help you to know more about your customers and what they are buying. Image analytics can help you to answer:

- What and how many photographs contain our brand name?
- Who are the customers that use our products?
- How do we increase the security and improve access control?

How do I use it?

Obviously in order to use image analytics you need to have images to analyse. If you do have images or you already do have recorded video footage of your stores or premises then you could use that video footage as your source data. Alternatively, if you have access to other images such as medical images then you could use image analytics to extract insights. Of course there are tight laws around the use of data including images, so you will need to be mindful not to infringe on those laws.

Although image analytics can be incredibly useful in detecting patterns or anomalies in medical images and face recognition can be used for security and customer insight it's probably not that appropriate for most businesses.

If you want to know more about the various image analytics techniques you can explore the links on page 40. Alternatively there are commercially available image analytics tools on the market that can help you.

Practical example

Casinos are currently using image analytics to identify high rollers for special treatment and presumably to identify people they want to keep out of their casinos, too. In Japan, grocery stores even use this technology to classify shoppers and blacklist serial complainers or shoplifters.

The biggest concern, especially around face recognition, is that it can be used without the person's knowledge or consent. From a safe distance someone can covertly identify an individual by name which then connects to intimate details about that person such as home address, dating preferences, employment history and religious beliefs. In 2011 researchers at Carnegie Mellon reported that this was not a hypothetical risk when they used a face recognition app to identify some students on campus by name, linking them to their public Facebook profiles and, in some cases, to their Social Security numbers.

It is especially potent because of the internet. There is now so much image data online that businesses don't even need to hold that data themselves for it to be useful. It is possible therefore to use image analytics to effectively scan the internet to gain insights and information about your customers and what offers or promotions they may respond to. In many ways image analytics represents a brave new world and it may only be a matter of time before legislation adds more controls and consumer safeguards.

Tips and traps

Like all analytics, image analytics is only really going to be useful if it helps to answer key strategic questions that you have as a business.

The biggest trap is privacy. Just because you can get your hands on images to analyse doesn't necessarily mean you should, or that what you are doing is ethical. Make sure you have a specific reason for using image analytics that is morally defensible and where the outcome will deliver additional value to your customers.

Further reading and references

For more on image analytics see for example:

- Baughman, A., Gao, J. and Pan, J.-Y. (eds) (2015) *Multimedia Data Mining and Analytics: Disruptive Innovation*, New York: Springer
- http://www.analytics-magazine.org/november-december-2011/694-images-a-videos-really-big-data
- http://www.springer.com/computer/image+processing/journal/11493
- http://www.theguardian.com/technology/2014/may/04/facial-recognition-technology-identity-tesco-ethical-issues

Video analytics

What is it?

Video analytics is the process of extracting information, meaning and insights from video footage. Of course video analytics can do everything that image analytics can do plus a bit more.

Whereas image analytics looks at a still image – either that of a photograph or medical scan and seeks to find patterns, anomalies or identify faces in the pictures – video analytics can also measure and track behaviour.

Traditionally, video data was only really gathered on CCTV for security purposes to monitor retail or business premises for shoplifting, malicious damage or employee wrongdoing. The purpose of the video footage was to protect the business and provide evidence if something happened. If nothing happened the recordings would be erased so the tape or digital hard drive could be re-used over and over again. All that data wasn't saved because a) there was too much of it and b) there was no way to use it.

But again all that has changed. Increases in storage capability and analytics techniques mean that all that video footage is now very useful.

Video analytics can now be used for:

- identification (face recognition);
- behaviour analysis;
- situation awareness.

When do I use it?

You may want to consider using video analytics if you want to know more about who is visiting your store or premises and what they are doing when they get there.

Face recognition can maintain security and also you can use face recognition (see Chapter 10) to find out more about your customers. But because video data is dynamic, not static like image data, you can also use it to monitor your customers' behaviour and learn more about how they react to offers, etc. It is, for example, now possible to collect data from different CCTV cameras in a retail environment, upload that data to a cloud server without additional infrastructure costs and analyse the footage to see how your customers behave and how they move through the store.

This data can help you to see how many people stop at a particular product display or offer for example, how long they engage with it and whether or not it is working and converting into sales.

You could also use video analytics to reduce costs, risk and assist decision making. For example, there is now software that allows you to automatically monitor a location 24/7; that video footage is then analysed using video and behavioural analytics solution and alerts you in real time to any abnormal and suspicious activity. Once installed and provided with the initial video feed, the software observes its environment, learns to distinguish normal behaviour from abnormal behaviour and sends relevant, real-time alerts to security personnel. The system is also self-correcting, which means that it continuously refines its own assumptions about behaviour and no human effort is required to define its parameters.

What business questions is it helping me to answer?

Video analytics can be incredibly useful in business to increase security and understand more about customer behaviour. It can help you to answer:

- Who is using our product (e.g. brand scanning in YouTube videos)?
- How effective is our shop/warehouse/airport/etc., layout?
- How can we analyse the behaviour and performance of our employees?
- How can we improve security?

How do I use it?

In order to use video analytics you need video footage. Most businesses, especially in a retail environment, already have this data but they don't use it behind the basic security backup should something go wrong.

If you already have this data then you may want to consider applying some analytics so you can use it more effectively. Plus because of advances in data storage and technology like cloud computing you don't need to invest a great deal more in order to yield some really powerful insights. Data from multiple CCTV cameras can easily be uploaded to a cloud server for analysis and insight that can help you to deliver better service and provide more enticing offers that your customers respond to.

If, for example, you have a display in your store but no one is stopping at it or picking up the product, you can see this within a matter of days and change the display until it does work.

If you want to know more about video analytics and how to use them you can explore the links at the end of this chapter. Alternatively there are many commercially available video analytics tools and providers on the market that can help you.

Practical examples

I worked with a global retailer to help them utilise video analytics more effectively. Originally they approached me to help them discover how long their customers waited in a queue because they wanted to reduce the waiting time at the till.

We were able to answer this question by using the CCTV footage that was already being recorded. Prior to our involvement each CCTV camera in every store had its own database and it would record the images for a week and then overwrite those images with new footage. Realising that this data held far greater value than simply preventing theft, the retailer decided to connect all the cameras in all its stores to one big cloud database that holds all the CCTV camera data. Specialist software then puts it all together to recognise movement and patterns as well as face recognition. Not only was the retailer able to identify how long people were waiting to queue and reduce that wait time, it was also able to combine all the images from different cameras to see how individuals walked through the store, which aisles they visited and which promotions were working and which ones were not.

Another customer of mine is Prozone, a leader in sports analytics. They collect data gathered from a number of cameras placed around a football or hockey pitch, for example, and track players. The system creates over 10 data-points per second for each player on the field and allows coaches to analyse all activities, on and off the ball, to answer questions like: miles covered by each player, successful and unsuccessful passes or tackles for each player, and even which players best attract opposition players away thus creating new spaces and attacking opportunities?

Video analytics can also assist decision making in complex, highly fluid situations such as aviation, air traffic control, ship navigation, power plant operation and emergency services. Using technology and video footage to alert personnel to changes or anomalies can also help to save lives and prevent crime.

Tips and traps

This type of analytics where it can all happen without a person's permission is currently a grey area in law. But there will come a time when it won't be, so always deliver best practice, treat all data with respect and privacy and ensure that if you are using your customers' video data then you are making sure the outcome is ethical and adds value to them not just your business.

The traps, as with image data, are the privacy issues and you need to make extra sure you stay on the right side of the law and use the data wisely and ethically.

Further reading and references

To understand more about video analytics see for example:

- Distante, C., Battiato, S. and Cavallaro, A. (eds) *Video Analytics for Audience Measurement: First International Workshop, VAAM 2014, Stockholm, Sweden, August 24, 2014. Revised Selected Papers*, New York: Springer
- http://www.eetimes.com/document.asp?doc_id=1273834
- http://www.bsia.co.uk/

Voice analytics

12

What is it?

Voice analytics, also known as speech analytics, is the process of extracting information, meaning and insights from audio recordings of conversations.

This form of analytics can analyse the topics or actual words and phrases being discussed in a conversation. This can be extremely useful for security purposes and certainly counter terrorist units inside most governments monitor a lot more of our conversation than we might imagine in order to identify people talking about things that they either shouldn't be talking about or to help identify potential treats.

Voice analytics can also be used to analyse the emotional content of the conversation above and beyond the actual words and phrases being discussed. When we get angry, for example, the pitch and tone of our voice changes, this is also true for most of us when we lie and so voice analytics can identify these changes in emotional state.

When do I use it?

All businesses need to keep their customers happy if they want to stay in business and stay ahead of the competition. If you have a product or service that requires technical assistance or you have large customer service call centres then this type of analytics can be really useful in maintaining and building ongoing customer relationships as well as highlight issues that need to be addressed.

You could, for example, use voice analytics to help identify recurring themes around customer complaints or recurring technical issues. These insights could help you to spot these potential pitfalls quicker and solve them before your customers take to social media to complain.

Voice analytics can also be used to help you identify when your customers are getting upset. By analysing the pitch and intonations of conversations taking place in your call centre you can gauge the emotional state of your customers and intervene earlier when they are getting angry or frustrated. The amount of speech and location of speech versus silence, i.e. call hold times or periods of silence, can also help customer-facing businesses provide better service and keep their customers happier. As a result, the conversations we've been told 'may be recorded for training purposes' can actually be used for training *and* provide useful insights instead of being lost or recorded over.

This type of analytics is also very useful in helping to identify underperforming customer service representatives so they can receive additional training or coaching, and can automatically monitor the level of customer service provided on calls, i.e. does the emotional customer end the call still upset or are they calmer and much happier? This is important information for customer retention and loyalty building.

What business questions is it helping me to answer?

Voice analytics can help you to answer:

- What do customers really think about our brand/product?
- How can we identify the customers that are upset and likely to leave?
- How can we identify lies (used in police forces and border agencies)?
- How can we make our operations more efficient (and cut down on, for example, form filling)?

How do I use it?

Voice analytic tools can spot spoken keywords, phrases or emotional tonality either as real-time alerts on live audio or as a post-processing step on recorded speech. It is actually this type of analytic ability that helps live TV and radio shows manage the unpredictability of guests. Obviously it's important that people don't swear on live shows, especially before the watershed, so voice analytics can help to recognise speech patterns that may be leading up to swearing and cut that person off before any damage is done.

Clearly if you want to use voice analytics you need to have voice data to analyse either as live audio or recorded conversations. And the more recent that data is the better, certainly for ongoing extraction of commercially relevant insights. The most obvious source of voice data is from call centres or customer services departments which are interacting with customers all the time.

In more cases, certainly within large businesses, this data will already exist and customers in call waiting queues are usually told that the conversation may be recorded. If this data already exists then it makes sense to use it more constructively in order to discover strategically significant information about products, processes, operational issues, areas for improvement and customer service performance. Voice analytics can provide you with information about what your customers really think about your company, products and services without much additional investment in market research. It is essentially about leveraging data you already have.

If you don't currently record your customer conversations then you may want to start. Technology for recording conversations is very common and inexpensive and so long as you tell your customers that the calls are or may be recorded then you can use that data to extract additional value from a service that you are already providing.

If you want to know more about voice analytics and how they can be used you can explore the links at the end of this chapter. Alternatively there are commercially available voice analytics tools and providers that can help you.

Practical example

Voice analytics can be used to extract value from what's being said and how it's being said in a way that simply wasn't possible a decade ago.

There are many social and commercial applications for voice analytics because it can help us to identify when someone is stressed, scared, happy, sad, or even when they are lying.

For example, voice analytics is already being used by insurance companies to help detect insurance fraud. If someone calls up a claims line and tells a representative about a new claim for a car accident or damage claim on their home then this type of analytics will help to detect who is lying and trying to commit insurance fraud. Insurance fraud is a huge ongoing problem for the industry that customers often end up paying for through increased premiums. Voice analytics is helping to identify the cheats, which will hopefully help everyone else.

As well as providing useful business insights voice analytics can be seen commercially in voice recognition software for dictaphones and smartphone dictation apps.

Plus it is this analytic capability that you are using when you talk to Siri on Apple's iPhone or Microsoft's Cortana which is available on new Nokia phones. By talking into your smart device the technology will decipher what you said and either take you to a specific website or remind you to send a birthday card to your friend. Also many modern cars offer a text-to-voice feature so that if you get a text message to your phone the car will convert the text to speech so you can hear your message without disrupting your driving.

Tips and traps

For voice analytics to be truly effective and useful the voice data needs to be clear and crisp so make sure you invest in quality equipment. And use the data to answer specific strategic questions and seek constant improvement rather than just seeing what the data tells you.

Recording conversations can make people nervous. For employees it can feel like a 'big brother' intervention that is designed to monitor what they are doing and saying. It is important therefore that any decision to record calls is positioned correctly for both the customers and the employees. Be sure to share the insights you learn with your people so they can appreciate that you are not listening to their every call but listening to what's going on behind the call.

Plus you can't record people without their permission so you need to tell your customers and employees that they are being recorded and allow them to opt out if they want to. Make sure you stay apprised of any changes to the law that could affect voice data and always err on the side of ethical caution.

Further reading and references

To find out more about voice analytics and how they can be used see for example:

- http://www.brainfoodextra.com/7236/analytics-and-call-centresmust-have-capability
- http://www.callcentrehelper.com/what-to-look-for-when-buying-speech-analytics-32315.htm
- http://www.mycustomer.com/feature/data-experience/how-use-speech-analytics-shape-your-contact-centre-kpis/166616

Monte Carlo simulation 13

What is it?

The Monte Carlo simulation is a mathematical problem-solving and risk assessment technique that approximates the probability of certain outcomes, and therefore the risk of certain outcomes, using computerised simulations of random variables.

The probability-based technique is used in fields such as finance, project management, manufacturing, engineering, research and development, insurance, oil and gas and transportation. It is useful for any industry or business that needs to assess risk of a future strategy or plan.

When you are seeking to forecast or predict the future to assess risk you need to make some assumptions around that scenario. For example, if you want to forecast the return on investment on your share portfolio you will need to make assumptions about the economy, return on investment and perhaps some assumptions about the businesses or markets where you hold shares. If you want to forecast the implications of moving premises or building a new plant then you will need to make assumptions around how long it will take, the impact it will have on business and the cost of borrowing, etc. Obviously these are often little more than educated guesses. There is no certainty around these assumptions and yet the assumptions that are made can massively impact the result.

The Monte Carlo simulation allows you to estimate ranges of values instead of a single guess. This creates a far more realistic picture of what might happen in the future. For example, you could estimate that the new plant will be ready in 12 months, 14 months, 16 months or 24 months. As such, this technique provides the decision maker with a range of possible outcomes and the probabilities of each outcome for any choice of action.

The technique is named after the casino-rich resort town of Monaco. It was first used by scientists working on the atom bomb and since the Second World War it has been used to model a variety of physical and conceptual systems.

When do I use it?

You could use the Monte Carlo simulation if you want to better understand the implications and ramifications of a particular course of action or decision.

It is especially useful when there is a high degree of uncertainty around some of the assumptions you need to make. For example, if you were considering launching a new product there are many unknown variables to consider. You don't really know how long the product will take to perfect, you don't know how long it will take to manufacture the product and iron out the glitches. Where many of the assumptions you need to make fall within a range rather than being a best-guess assumption you are confident in then the Monte Carlo simulation could help limit the risk so you are able to execute the strategy with more certainty and awareness of the best-case and worst-case scenarios.

In essence this technique illustrates the extreme possibilities that could occur. Looking at the implications from worst-case scenario through the middle ground and into best-case scenario, along with the probability of each of those scenarios happening you get a much better idea of the risks and rewards of your proposed intervention.

What business questions is it helping me to answer?

Monte Carlo simulation can help the decision maker to get a much clearer, broader understanding of the risks and rewards of a particular course of action. It can help you to answer:

- Which product should we launch next?
- Which investments will yield the highest returns?
- Should we acquire this company or not?
- How long is a complex project or programme likely to take or cost?

How do I use it?

If you are using a Monte Carlo simulation you are building a model of possible outcomes by substituting a range of values known as a probability distribution for any unknown or uncertain factor. The result of the model is recorded, and the process is repeated over and over again. Depending on the number of uncertainties within the simulation and the ranges specified for them, the simulation can involve hundreds, thousands or even tens of thousands of calculations. Each simulation calculates the model using different randomly selected values.

When the simulation is complete there will be a large number of results from the model, each based on random input values. These results are used to describe the likelihood of the variables actually happening. And the Monte Carlo simulation produces distributions of possible outcome values, which can aid decision making and help lower risk.

If you want to know more about Monte Carlo simulation and an example of how it works explore the links at the end of this chapter. This technique can be run using Microsoft Excel (again, many easy to follow tutorials can be found online) or you can purchase software to help you.

Practical example

Say you have an upcoming project and you really need to know how it's going to pan out because the success of the project has far-reaching consequences for your business and therefore your career.

A normal forecasting model would start with some fixed estimates around a number of variables but you don't feel suitably confident that the fixed estimates are correct. There are three parts to the project and each must be completed before the project is finalised, so in a normal forecasting model there would be three fixed estimates and a total estimate. You would feel happier if you could also figure out the likelihood that your estimates were correct. The Monte Carlo simulation allows you to do that because you can enter a range of completion times to cover the best- and worst-case scenarios for the completion of the project.

The simulation will then run and provide you with the probability for each variable. So, for example, if you thought the total completion time would be 15 months the Monte Carlo simulation would tell you that there was a 42 per cent chance of completion in 15 months and there was an 82 per cent chance it would be finished in 18 months. That sort of insight and understanding can certainly help to manage the project and determine the impact of those additional three months that you hadn't accounted for.

The key feature of a Monte Carlo simulation is that it can assess ranges of variables and, perhaps most importantly, the likelihood of each estimate or assumption in that range actually happening. And that can give you a significantly better understanding of the risk and uncertainty involved.

Tips and traps

Like any forecasting model or predictive technique the Monte Carlo simulation is only as good as the estimates and assumptions you put in. Use your past experience, historical results and expertise to create a realistic and plausible range to test.

Remember, the simulation only represents probabilities and not certainty, but it is still a powerful tool for helping to navigate an unknown future.

Further reading and references

To learn more about Monte Carlo simulation see for example:

- Carsey, T.M. and Harden, J.J. (2013) *Monte Carlo Simulation and Resampling Methods for Social Science*, 1st edition, London: SAGE Publications

- Glasserman, P. (2003) 'Monte Carlo Methods in Financial Engineering', *Stochastic Modelling and Applied Probability* 53 (August)
- http://www.palisade.com/risk/monte_carlo_simulation.asp
- http://www.projectsmart.co.uk/docs/monte-carlo-simulation.pdf
- http://www.riskamp.com/files/RiskAMP%20-%20Monte%20Carlo%20Simulation.pdf

Linear programming 14

Linear programming, also known as linear optimisation, is a method of identifying the best outcome based on a set of constraints using a linear mathematical model.

It allows you to solve problems involving minimising and maximising conditions such as how to maximise profit while minimising costs. For example, taking the limitations of materials and labour you could use linear programming to determine the 'best' production levels in order to maximise profits under those conditions.

It was originally developed in 1937 by Leonid Kantorovich during the Second World War as a way to plan expenditures and returns so as to reduce costs to the army while maximising the losses incurred by the enemy. The method was kept secret until 1947 when it was simplified by George Dantzig and moved out beyond the military.

Today, linear programming is used extensively in various fields including business, economics and engineering to identify the optimum solution among various linear relationships and constraints.

Linear programming is part of a very important and useful area of mathematics called optimisation techniques. Clearly being able to optimise your resources is an important skill in successful business and beyond.

As such you would use linear programming if you have a number of constraints such as time, raw materials, labour, profit margin and you wanted to know the best combination or where to direct your resources for maximum profit.

Linear programming is essentially a resource allocation process that can help guide decision making and increase revenue.

It is possible to model many diverse types of problems such as planning, scheduling, routing, assignment and design using linear programming. Industries that use this technique effectively include transportation, energy, telecommunications, and manufacturing.

What business questions is it helping me to answer?

Linear programming can help you to decide how best to allocate your resources to maximise your outcomes. It can help you to answer:

- How do I best allocate resources to optimise processes?
- How do I best deploy resources to maximise returns?
- What is the optimal delivery route, given our constraints?
- What is the optimal level of energy to use to maximise output?

How do I use it?

The first step in linear programming is to define your control variables (typically quantities of X and Y). You then need to define the objective function. In other words identify what you are trying to maximise or minimise. Next you need to write the constraints as inequalities in terms of the control variables. And finally solve the problem graphically.

The resulting graph visualises the inequalities, known as constraints, to form a 'walled-off' area on the x,y-plane. This walled-off area is called the 'feasibility region', which then allows you to figure out the coordinates of the corners of this feasibility region. This is done by finding the intersection points of the various pairs of lines. Once you know those you test these corner points using the optimisation equation to identify the highest or lowest value.

If you want to know more about linear programming and how to use it you can explore the links at the end of this chapter. Alternatively there are software tools available that can help.

Practical example

The following example and graphs were sourced from http://www.thestudentroom .co.uk/wiki/revision:linear_programming. Say you run a manufacturing plant making two main products – product X and product Y. You only have so many employees on the production lines and the production lines are only able to make one product at a time. There are only so many employees capable of working so many hours and the raw materials used to make each product are the same yet the sale price and units sold are different.

You're not really sure how you should allocate the various resources in your factory. You use your expertise and look at historic data to help, but you can't help feeling that there has to be a better way and decide to use linear programming to help direct your decision making.

You're controllable variables are product X and product Y. And your objective function is to figure out how to maximise your profit. And you identify your constraints:

- product X takes 6 hours to create and generates £12 profit;
- product Y takes 4 hours to create and generates £6 profit;
- due to various limitations the most of either that can be produced is 400 units;
- there are 1,700 assembly hours available.

The resulting feasibility region is shown on the following graph:

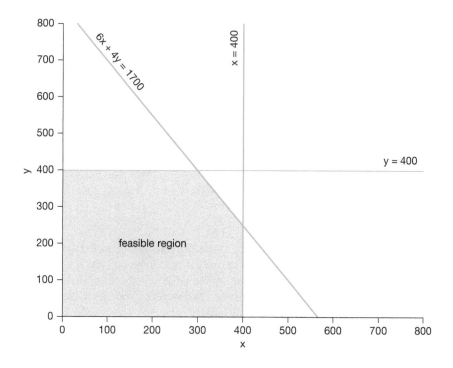

You know that profit is maximised at one of the corners of the feasibility region. To establish which one draw on a line with the gradient of the objective function and move the line closer to the feasibility region. Whichever corner the line hits first is where profit will be maximised.

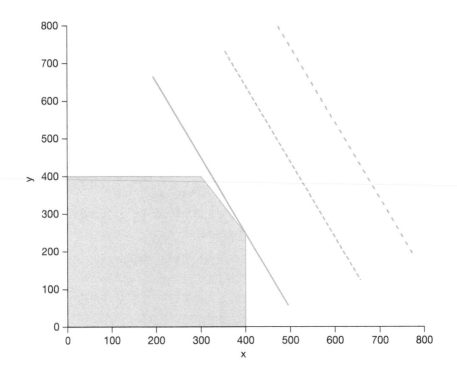

In the second example graph the objective line hits the feasibility region at the corner point of the intersection of 400 and 250. This means that in order to maximise your profit with the resources you have you need to produce 400 product X and 250 product Y giving you a profit of £6,300.

Tips and traps

In the production process it is very easy for bottlenecks to occur and it's always a constant dance to figure out how best to use the resources you have. If you don't watch production closely, machines can lie idle while others are overused. Linear programming can help you to highlight these challenges so you can make the most of what you have.

Of course it is only really useful for problems that can be expressed as linear equations (represent a straight line). Not all constraints are as helpful, in which case linear programming will not work. Plus there are always other factors that you may need to take into consideration such as weather conditions or wider market conditions. Use it as a decision-making tool but don't rely on the results totally without considering how other uncertain factors could impact those results.

Further reading and references

To learn more about linear programming see for example:

- Sultan, A. (2011) *Linear Programming: An Introduction With Applications*, 2nd edition, CreateSpace Independent Publishing Platform
- Gass, S. I. (2010) *Linear Programming: Methods and Applications*, 5th edition, Mineola, NY: Dover Publications
- http://www.math.ucla.edu/~tom/LP.pdf
- http://www.purplemath.com/modules/linprog.htm
- http://www.princeton.edu/~achaney/tmve/wiki100k/docs/Linear_programming.html
- http://www.thestudentroom.co.uk/wiki/revision:linear_programming

15 Cohort analysis

What is it?

Cohort analysis is a subset of behavioural analytics which allows you to study the behaviour of a group over time. The groups or cohorts in this context are aggregations of data points, or relevant stakeholders in your business, and the data may come from e-commerce platforms, web applications or sales data.

The groups being analysed usually share a common characteristic so that you can compare cohorts and extract some potentially meaningful insights. The behaviour being assessed can be anything that is of interest to you and your business.

The goal of any business analytic tool is to analyse data and extract actionable and commercially relevant information that the business can use to increase results or performance. But a database full of hundreds of thousands of entries relating to all users, across many different categories and time spans can make it difficult to extract much in the way of useful insights. The universe of data is too large and too jumbled.

What makes this technique so useful is that it allows you to see patterns in the data more clearly – patterns that would otherwise be missed if the data was not clustered in cohorts. By drilling down into each specific cohort you can gain a much better understanding of that group's behaviour. Obviously when you understand what a specific cohort or group is doing you can modify your approach to improve results.

When do I use it?

Cohort analysis is especially useful if you want to know more about the behaviour of a group of your stakeholders such as customers or employees.

Rather than having to take a broad brush look at what all your customers are doing or how they are reacting to a new product or change in service, or, for example, looking at absenteeism across all your employees, you can get a much more accurate picture of what's really going on if you can divide those stakeholders into groups that share similar features.

Cohort analysis is therefore more commercially relevant and can help you identify problems and make better decisions.

What business questions is it helping me to answer?

Cohort analysis can help guide decision making, especially around decisions that could alter behaviour in important stakeholder groups. It can help you to answer:

- Who are my most profitable customers?
- What characteristics do my different customer groups share in common?
- How do particular groups of my customers behave?
- What characteristics do particular groups of employees share in common?

How do I use it?

There are four essential steps in cohort analysis:

1   You need to determine what questions you want answered. What are you trying to find out about your stakeholder group or sub-groups? The whole point of analysis of any type is to provide answers to strategically important questions so you can identify what needs to be done differently or what opportunity needs to be exploited in order to improve some element of your business.

2   Next you need to define the metrics that will be able to help you answer the questions you've identified. Cohort analysis requires the identification of the specific properties you are going to examine in the group. For example, gender, date of first or last purchase, level of purchase, etc.

3   Next you need to define or identify the specific cohorts you are going to assess. This will often require you to perform attribute contribution in order to find the relevant differences between each group or sub-group so that you can use that difference to explain the difference in their behaviour.

4   Finally you perform the cohort analysis. The findings are often then visualised in a graph or table. This visualisation can help spot the patterns that will then shape decision making.

There are many different variations on cohort analysis that you can run based on your needs and what you are trying to understand. If you want to know more about cohort analysis and how to use it explore the links at the end of this chapter. Plus there are many software options available that could help you.

Practical example

Perhaps you want to know more about who is buying your products. You can look at sales data to see how many sales you've made and you can look through demographic data, but if you looked at all the data as one data set if wouldn't necessarily be obvious if you were selling more to one market segment than another.

Cohort analysis allows you to create and assess the sub-groups or cohorts that exist within the single large data set called 'customers' and drill down to see if there are any additional insights that could improve your results.

You might, for example, discover that you have groups or cohorts that outsell all the other groups combined. If you discover that most of your sales are made to women between 35 and 45 then you can tailor your marketing and advertising to further tap into that lucrative market and increase sales.

Tips and traps

Cohort studies are based on past result data or what your group under investigation did in the past. This can be a trap because what happened before will not necessarily happen in the future.

Further reading and references

To find out more about cohort analysis see for example:

- Norval, G. (2005) *Cohort Analysis (Quantitative Applications in the Social Sciences)*, 2nd edition, London: SAGE Publications
- http://www.thedeerinitiative.co.uk/uploads/guides/108.pdf
- http://www.nanigans.com/2014/04/21/how-to-use-cohort-analysis-to-find-your-most-valuable-ads/
- http://www.youtube.com/watch?v=NyhVdGmnh0l

Factor analysis 16

What is it?

Factor analysis is the collective name given to a group of statistical techniques that are used primarily for data reduction and structure detection. In modern business we are inundated with data. New data, old data, new types and formats of data – we are literally drowning in the stuff. And having too much data can be just as useless and debilitating as having too little.

Factor analysis can reduce the number of variables within data to help make it more useful. This reduction in variables within the data also makes it much easier to detect a structure in the relationships between those variables which makes the variables easier to classify.

This is made possible because of a key concept – that multiple observed variables have similar patterns of responses because they are all associated with a latent variable, i.e. a variable that isn't or can't be measured. For example, people are likely to respond similarly to questions about personal income, education and occupation because those questions are all associated with the latent variable of socioeconomic status.

It originated in psychometrics and is often used in behavioural and social sciences, marketing, product management and operations research. It is particularly useful when you have large quantities of data to analyse and draw insight from.

When do I use it?

You would consider using factor analysis if you need to analyse and understand more about the interrelationships among a large number of variables and to explain these variables in terms of their common underlying dimensions or factors.

For example, if you have gathered a treasure trove of quantitative and qualitative data about your customers and what they think and feel about your product offerings, this is potentially very useful. But only if you can unravel the interdependencies and appreciate what variables affect what outcome. This can be very difficult when there are a lot of potential variables and a lot of potential outcomes.

Factor analysis can help, condensing the information contained in a number of original variables into a smaller set of dimensions (factors) with a minimum loss of information.

What business questions is it helping me to answer?

Factor analysis can help you extract insights from huge data sets. It can also help you to identify causal relationships that could direct strategy and improve decision making. It can help you to answer:

- What factors have my least loyal customers in common?
- What are the factors that make our youngest customers buy our product?
- What factors are associated with high staff turnover?

How do I use it?

Say you were going to use factor analysis for marketing purposes; there are four basic steps:

1. Identify the relevant attributes your customers use to evaluate your products in any product category. Anything from five to 20 attributes can be chosen such as colour, size, weight, price, ease of use, etc.

2. Use quantitative market research techniques (Chapter 19) to collect data from a sample of your customers to establish how important they rate your identified attributes.

3. Input the data into a statistical program such as SAS or SPSS and run the factor analysis process. The program will then yield a set of underlying interdependencies between the attributes or factors. For example, colour may positively influence sales, or weight may negatively influence sales.

4. Use these factors to improve your products and or marketing message.

If you want to know more about factor analysis and how to use it you can explore the links at the end of this chapter. Alternatively there are many commercially available factor analysis tools on the market that can help you.

Practical example

Factor analysis can be used to improve employee engagement because it allows you to analyse the structure of the interrelationships or correlations among a large number of variables by defining a set of common underlying dimensions, known as factors.

If you realise that your staff turnover is too high but you are unsure why, you may conduct exit interviews and initiate an employee survey. But the data alone may not tell you very clearly what is happening in the business. By identifying all the salient attributes that you can think of that may be causing the high turnover you can then use factor analysis to assess the correlations and identify patterns that can help you to solve or at least reduce the problem.

This is particularly useful because both objective and subjective attributes can be used provided the subjective attributes can be converted into scores. Often in issues such as staff turnover or high absenteeism it's the qualitative subjective data that holds the key to solving the issue. This technique can also identify relationships and latent dimensions or constraints that direct analysis may not.

Tips and traps

So long as you have the right statistical program factor analysis is very accessible. It's easy and inexpensive.

That said, its ultimate usefulness depends heavily on the researchers' ability to collect a sufficient and relevant set of attributes. If important attributes are missed or ignored then the value of the analysis is significantly compromised and may lead to poor decision making.

Further reading and references

To learn more about factor analysis and how to use it see for example:

- Walkey, F. and Welch, G. (2010) *Demystifying Factor Analysis: How It Works and How To Use It*, Xlibris Corp.
- Gorsuch, R.L. (2014) *Factor Analysis: Classic Edition*, 2nd edition, Abingdon: Routledge
- Garson, G.D. (2013) *Factor Analysis*, Asheboro, NC: Statistical Associates Publishers
- http://www.statsoft.com/textbook/principal-components-factor-analysis
- http://www.hawaii.edu/powerkills/UFA.HTM
- http://www.theanalysisfactor.com/factor-analysis-1-introduction/

17 Neural network analysis

What is it?

In order to understand what neural network analysis is we need first to know what a neural network is. Essentially, a neural network is a computer program modelled on the human brain which can process a huge amount of information and identify patterns in a similar way that we do. Many neural networks also learn as they process like we do and as such they improve over time.

Neural network analysis is therefore the process of analysing the mathematical modelling that makes up a neural network. This analytics technique is particularly useful if you have a large amount of data. Because neural networks recognise patterns and learn to improve their recognition ability, their insights can help make predictions. These predications can then be tested and the results used to improve decision making and performance.

Neural networks are already widely used in industries such as banking, fraud prevention, medicine and manufacturing.

When do I use it?

This type of analysis can be applied to many different systems of data in a wide variety of fields. In business, neural network analysis can help you improve sales forecasting, customer research, and target marketing. Analysis of neural networks can also be helpful in streamlining manufacturing processes and assessing risk.

It can also be used to determine the effectiveness of a neural network's ability to learn. Remember, a neural network is designed to mimic the learning and pattern recognition features of the human brain so the results of the analysis can be checked against the results interpreted by a human user to see how close they are. This can guide the ongoing development of the neural network making it more and more useful and more and more accurate.

Whether helping people to solve statistical problems or creating simulations of complex environments for testing, the analysis is an essential part of making a neural network increasingly useful. There is little doubt that as they advance and evolve, the uses for them will continue to grow.

What business questions is it helping me to answer?

Neural network analysis can help to forecast the future and process large quantities of data. It can help you to answer:

- What products are our customers likely to buy?
- How many products are we likely to sell, especially across a complete portfolio of products with cross-effects?
- What variables influence the buying decision of our customers?
- What is the optimal allocation of advertising expenses?
- Where do we have bottlenecks in our manufacturing process?

How do I use it?

First you need to decide what problem you are trying to solve using a neural network and then gather data for training purposes. Essentially you need to train the neural network to process data and decipher patterns so that the result is constantly improving as the network learns.

Ideally the training data set should include a number of cases, each containing values for a range of input and output variables. You will need to decide what variables to use, and which and how many cases to gather.

Initially your choice of variables will be guided by your own experience of the problem area you are seeking answers on. Let your intuition guide you regarding which input variables are likely to be influential. Include the ones you think have the most impact and test to see if you are correct. Re-test until you whittle down the variables.

If you want to know more about neural network analysis and how to use it you can explore the links at the end of this chapter. Alternatively there are software tools and providers that can help you. These software tools will break down the results of the neural network analysis thus allowing you to make very accurate predictions by presenting the data in an easily digestible and understandable format.

The software may also allow the user to test out the changes that the analysis recommends to make sure that the initial prediction holds true.

Practical example

Neural networks are already used to create models of the human body which allow healthcare professionals to test out the results of certain medical interventions before they are conducted in the real world. This is of course incredibly useful and potentially lifesaving. These simulations then provide additional information that can help doctors make the right decisions.

Google's Science Fair grand prize was actually won by an American teenager who used neural networks to create an app that can accurately diagnose breast cancer in biopsy tissue 99 per cent of the time. With no medical training Brittaney Wenger created the app using a vast amount of different data points, and the neural network is able to learn and detect patterns that can't be detected by the human eye. For years doctors have found it incredibly difficult to diagnose breast cancer based on a biopsy but Wenger's program is set to change breast cancer diagnosis forever.[1]

Tips and traps

Neural network analysis is a complex analytics methodology that normally requires the input from experts in neural network analysis as well as the use of specialist software.

Further reading and references

To find out more about neural network analysis see for example:

- http://mitpress.mit.edu/books/mathematical-methods-neural-network-analysis-and-design
- http://www.wisegeek.com/what-is-neural-network-analysis.htm
- http://metalab.uniten.edu.my/~chensd/courses/Neural%20Network%20in%20MATLAB.pdf
- http://www.statsoft.com/Textbook/Neural-Networks
- http://www.ijcsit.com/docs/Volume%205/vol5issue01/ijcsit20140501140.pdf

---

[1]BBC Two *Horizon*, 'Monitor Me' narrated by Dr Kevin Fong (2013)

Meta-analytics – literature analysis

18

What is it?

Meta-analysis is the term that describes the synthesis of previous studies in an area in the hope of identifying patterns, trends or interesting relationships among the pre-existing literature and study results.

Meta-analysis is essentially the study of previous studies. For example, a meta-analysis of lung cancer would synthetise all the studies ever conducted on lung cancer into one meta-study. Often these meta-studies can provide a fuller, richer picture of the research area.

When do I use it?

You don't always have to conduct your own analysis to benefit from the analysis. If what you want to find out has been the topic of a number of studies then you can collate all the previous information into one meta study so that you can obtain the insights without conducting any of the original analysis yourself.

So long as the analysis is in the public domain or relatively easy to access this approach can be considerably cheaper than running your own analysis.

What business questions is it helping me to answer?

Meta-analytics can help you to answer:

- What are the trends in market X?
- How is customer behaviour likely to change over the coming years?
- What will be the role of mobile computing in our industry?
- What factors are most important for staff engagement?

How do I use it?

Conceptually a meta-analysis is a statistical approach that combines data from multiple sources to provide a broader, richer and potentially more accurate insight into the area being studied. If several existing studies disagree then meta-analysis can highlight these differences and determine the statistical likelihood of which findings are likely to be more accurate.

This can then allow you to generalise into a larger population so that you have a better and more accurate idea of what will happen in that larger population. Meta-analysis becomes more precise and accurate the more data is used, which can therefore yield more insights and they can be tested.

Practical example

Meta-analysis could be particularly useful if you were looking to enter into a new market or geographic territory. If you don't already operate in that market or territory then you may be tempted to make assumptions about buying behaviour and the suitability of your products or services to that market.

If however there have already been some studies conducted on this new market or territory – even if they are focused around different products or services – you could collate these studies and seek to identify patterns of behaviour that could influence your decision making and minimise the risk.

Tips and traps

The better the individual studies the better the meta-analysis. Sourcing and validating studies to include is therefore important but can be time-consuming. In addition if the studies have been badly designed then they can skew results. Only use robust studies that have been methodically designed.

The traps include bias that exists within each study – bias that you may or may not be aware of.

Further reading and references

To read more about meta-analytics see for example:

- Borenstein, M., Higgins, J.P.T. and Rothstein, H.R. (2009) *Introduction to Meta-Analysis*, 1st edition, Hoboken, NJ: Wiley
- Schmidt, F.L. and Hunter, J.Q. (2014) *Methods of Meta-Analysis: Correcting Error and Bias in Research Findings*, 3rd edition, London: SAGE Publications
- Cooper, H.M. (2009) *Research Synthesis and Meta-Analysis: A Step-by-Step Approach*, 4th edition, London: SAGE Publications
- http://www.ncbi.nlm.nih.gov/pmc/articles/PMC2121629/
- http://www.analytics20.org/meta-analytics/

[PART TWO]

Analytics input tools
or data collection methods

Quantitative surveys

19

What is it?

A quantitative survey seeks to 'quantify' something from a numerical or statistical point of view. It may be used to quantify the size of a market or market share, or it may be used to quantify opinion.

Quantitative surveys are characterised by their structure. They pose specific closed questions and then provide a selection of answers that the respondent must choose from. The respondent is not allowed to elaborate but instead must select the answer that is correct or most correct for them.

The standardised approach and structured answers make quantitative surveys easier to complete and interpret. If you need to classify features, count them, and then construct a statistical model to explain what you observed then you probably need to collect quantitative data collected automatically via operations, or through a well-designed survey.

Why does it matter?

It matters because quantitative survey data allows you to build up a clearer picture of how a random sample of a target population or audience behaves or what they think about a particular topic. The findings can then be projected out to the whole target audience to generalise opinion and measure the incidence of various views or opinions within the survey. This type of analysis can also be helpful in finding out more about particular sub-groups to understand more about what they want, like or dislike about your offering.

Plus if you initiate quantitative surveys on a regular basis to the same group of people then you can monitor changes to behaviour or opinion over time. This is especially useful if you maintain at least some of the same questions so you can make accurate comparisons.

How can I use it in practice?

Quantitative surveys and questionnaires are ideal if you want to quantify something whether that is opinion or the potential size of a market. They are especially useful in helping to:

- Establish whether or not there is a market for your products and services.
- Establish whether your audience is aware of your product or service.
- Estimate how many people are interested in buying your product or service and the likely size of your market.
- What type of people are your best customers.
- Establish your customer's buying habits.
- Figure out the changing needs of your target market.

Quantitative surveys are very flexible and they can be particularly useful for measuring strength of feeling regarding a particular area of interest such as customer satisfaction or how much a customer loves a product or service. It can also allow you to measure how that opinion changes over time, which can help to get back on track quicker.

They can, however, be quite easy to fudge – simply by skewing the recipient group. Plus, because of their flexibility, quantitative surveys are widely used which means respondents can be quite jaded about filling them in. You may need to provide an incentive to get enough people to participate to ensure it's worthwhile.

How do I get started?

You need to know what questions you are seeking answers to and design the survey around those strategically important questions.

There are some guidelines to remember when creating your survey:

- Surveys of any kind to any stakeholder group can induce eye-rolling and apathy so make sure you explain the purpose and potential benefit of the survey. If recipients understand why they are being asked to complete the survey and what difference the results might make to their lives then they are more inclined to engage with the questions, answer accurately and provide useful information.
- Use clear, simple language. That means no overly complex 'business-speak' or jargon.
- Ask one question at a time. Don't roll questions together. For example, don't ask recipients 'How attractive and easy to use is product X'? They are two different questions.
- Make it as short and easy to complete as possible. Only ask questions that you genuinely need the answers to.
- Have your survey professional designed so that it looks attractive and includes plenty of white space.

Once you have designed your survey consider distributing it online. Most quantitative surveys are conducted online via web-based surveys such as Survey Monkey to aid in the collection and analysis of results. They can also be conducted over the phone, by post or face to face but this tends to be more expensive because the results must then also be input into an analytics tool.

Possible data sources

The data comes directly from specially created quantitative surveys which can be sent to specific target groups such as your customers, your employees, suppliers, investors, etc.

These surveys can be administered face to face via interview or over the phone. Or they can be sent out through the post or conducted using online web-based or mobile tools.

How difficult or costly is it to collect?

This will depend on how big the survey is and how it's conducted. Obviously it will be more expensive if you decide to hire researchers to ask questions face to face or print and post a questionnaire with telephone follow-up. In postal survey's all the responses will also still need to be input into a program for analysis so this is usually an additional labour cost.

In most cases the most cost-effective and quickest approach to quantitative surveys is via an online web-based tool that distributes the survey and inputs responses directly into a program that will then analyse the results, or collate the data ready for export into a program that can analyse the data.

Practical example

A travel agent may want to know more about their customers so they can target their marketing initiatives to the right areas at the right time. They may create a customer survey which may ask a number of pertinent questions such as 'How many times have you flown overseas in the last 6 months?' The answers may be:

Never

1–2

2–5

6–10

More than 10

This structured approach allows the travel agent to analyse a large amount of data and convert that into useful statistics that can then be extrapolated to a wider population and help guide decision making and marketing activities.

Tips and traps

Define the target market of your survey very clearly so you know who you are seeking opinion from and why. Once you understand this then select the best contact method for that audience not for you. Unless it's easy and convenient for your target audience to complete the survey they won't bother, so remove as many obstacles as possible.

Don't make the survey too long. Only ask questions that you really need to know the answer to and seek to make completing the survey as quick and easy as possible for the recipient.

Further reading and references

To find out more about conducting quantitative surveys see for example:

- Dillman, D., Smith, J.D. and Christian, L.M. (2014) *Internet, Phone, Mail, and Mixed-Mode Surveys: The Tailored Design Method*, 4th edition, Hoboken, NJ: Wiley
- Fowler, F.J. (2013) *Survey Research Methods*, 5th edition, London: SAGE Publications
- http://www.marketingdonut.co.uk/marketing/market-research/questionnaires-surveys-and-focus-groups/what-is-quantitative-research-
- http://www.bl.uk/bipc/resmark/qualquantresearch/qualquantresearch.html
- http://www.ehow.com/how_7528860_analyze-quantitative-survey-results.html
- http://www.orau.gov/cdcynergy/soc2web/Content/activeinformation/tools/toolscontent/quantiativemethods.htm

Qualitative surveys

20

Where a quantitative survey seeks to 'quantify' a topic through numbers and statistics, a qualitative survey looks to 'qualify' the response with more subjective opinion. A qualitative survey helps you to understand the underlying reasons and motivations behind a target group's actions and behaviours.

For example, if you were thinking about changing your corporate livery or branding it would be wise to conduct some qualitative research beforehand to establish how strongly or otherwise your market felt about your current branding as well as the impressions and emotional reactions they have to the new branding.

Potentially you get access to much more nuanced and detailed information about how a target group thinks, feels and acts regarding a particular product or topic. Where quantitative surveys may tell you the percentage of your audience that hate your product or are unhappy with delivery changes, the qualitative survey will tell you why. It's the why that helps to define the problem and find appropriate solutions.

As a result, this type of research is particularly useful for identifying issues and helping to come up with ideas and hypotheses to test to solve those issues.

It is, however, more complex to analyse because the information that is provided is unstructured and does not tick a box or prescribe to any rules. This means that to extract useful insights from qualitative surveys you may have to invest in text-based analysis (see Chapter 8) or sentiment analysis (see Chapter 9).

Why does it matter?

It matters because qualitative surveys provide greater subjective input around a particular change, problem or topic.

They are not as structured as quantitative surveys because the real value comes from the ability of the respondents to say exactly what they want rather than select the best answer from a prescribed list.

This more detailed and personal information can help to really understand an issue from the respondent's point of view, help generate ideas for improvement, and uncover trends in thought and opinion.

How can I use it in practice?

Qualitative surveys and questionnaires are ideal for understanding more about how someone thinks and feels about a topic. They are by definition exploratory and are ideal when you don't know what you will discover.

They are especially useful if you want to know:

- What your customers think and feel about your product or service.
- How your customers decide between your different products or between you and your competition. What motivates them to choose you?
- How your branding, design and packaging influences your customers for and against certain products and services.
- What marketing messages or advertising has the most impact on your customers and prospects – both positively and negatively.
- How your pricing affects buying behaviour.

How do I get started?

As with quantitative surveys, you need to know what questions you are seeking answers to and design the survey around those strategically important questions.

The guidelines for quantitative surveys (see Chapter 19) are also relevant for qualitative surveys

Once you've designed your survey consider distributing it online. Most qualitative surveys are conducted online via web-based surveys such as Survey Monkey to aid in the collection and analysis of results. They can also be conducted over the phone, by post or face to face but this tends to be more expensive because the results must then also be input into an analytics tool.

Possible data sources

The data comes directly from specially created qualitative surveys.

These surveys can be administered face to face via interview or over the phone. Or they can be sent out through the post or conducted using online web-based or mobile tools.

How difficult or costly is it to collect?

This will depend on how big the survey is and how it's conducted. Like the quantitative survey it will be more expensive if you decide to hire researchers to ask questions face to face, print and post a questionnaire, or telephone respondents. In postal survey's all the responses will also still need to be input into a program for analysis so this is usually an additional labour cost.

The most cost-effective approach is to use an online web-based tool which distributes the survey and directly inputs responses into a program that will then collect the data for analysis and may also analyse it.

Practical example

Qualitative surveys are often used to help companies find out more about their customers. Say you notice on social media that a few of your customers are unhappy about the service your company is providing. There are a few derogatory tweets and Facebook posts. You're a smart business leader so you don't want to ignore these and are keen to figure out if this is just a few isolated incidents or an indication of a wider problem.

You could use a qualitative survey to tease out opinion so that you can isolate where the issues are and find a relevant solution. The challenge with qualitative surveys is that the questions are open-ended which means that the recipient can say whatever they want. Open-ended questions can yield open-ended answers that are not very useful. For example, if you asked, 'How was your last customer experience?' the recipient could potentially reply 'Good' or 'Terrible', but neither is terribly helpful. Whereas if you asked your customers to describe their last purchasing experience with your company you are likely to get much more insightful information.

In order to ask the right questions you need to have an idea of what the problem might be so pay attention to any signals you've already received regarding any customer unhappiness and seek to clarify if your assumptions are correct.

Tips and traps

Keep the survey small as the data gathered can be unwieldy.

As with all surveys only ask questions that are genuinely useful or relevant to the matter at hand. Don't be tempted to add more questions just because the answers 'might be interesting'. Figure out what you are trying to find out and ask only the questions that will answer those queries.

To save time, money and potential survey overkill many companies are now incorporating both qualitative and quantitative elements in their surveys. Allow recipients to provide additional feedback should they want to so they have the opportunity to raise issues that are important to them but do not appear as a specific question on the survey.

Further reading and references

To find out more about conducting qualitative surveys see for example:

- Patton, M.Q. (2001) *Qualitative Research & Evaluation Methods*, 3rd edition, London: SAGE Publications

- Merriam, S.B. (2009) *Qualitative Research: A Guide to Design and Implementation*, 3rd edition, San Francisco, CA: Jossey-Bass
- Dillman, D., Smith, J.D. and Christian, L.M. (2014) *Internet, Phone, Mail, and Mixed-Mode Surveys: The Tailored Design Method*, 4th edition, Hoboken, NJ: Wiley
- https://www.surveymonkey.com/blog/en/blog/2013/04/10/qualitative-vs-quantitative/
- http://www.qualitative-research.net/index.php/fqs/article/view/1450/2946
- http://www.ehow.com/how_7499465_analyze-qualitative-survey-results.html
- http://www.ons.gov.uk/ons/guide-method/method-quality/general-methodology/data-collection-methodology/what-is-qualitative-research-/index.html
- http://www.edu.plymouth.ac.uk/resined/Qualitative%20methods%202/qualrshm.htm

Focus groups

21

What is it?

A focus group is a form of qualitative research where a group of specially selected or randomly selected individuals come together to discuss a specific topic. Participants are usually recruited based on their demographics, psychographics, buying attitudes, or past buying behaviour.

The facilitator of the group is known as the moderator and he or she will ask questions and participants will answer the questions and/or discuss the issue with the other members while the moderator listens, makes notes and asks additional more probing questions.

There are several types of focus group:

- **Two-way focus group** – where one focus group watches another and discusses what they observe. This can be particularly useful if the topic is complex or challenging, as seeing what the other group thinks can open up new lines of discussion and new ideas.

- **Dual moderator focus group** – where each moderator has a different role: one to make sure the group runs smoothly and everyone has an opportunity to speak, and the other to make sure all the topics are covered. This can be particularly useful if there is a lot of ground to cover.

- **Duelling moderator focus group** – where two moderators deliberately take opposing sides in the discussion, playing the role of devil's advocate with each other. This is particularly useful when there appears to be one clear 'winner' or correct approach because it helps to shift the participants' view point and open up other ideas.

- **Respondent moderator focus group** – where one of the respondents is asked to act as the moderator temporarily. The answer to a question is often influenced by who asked the questions, appointing one of the group or inviting a participant to play the role of moderator can initiate new thinking and change the answers. This can be particularly useful if the group is running out of answers.

- **Client participant focus group** – where one or more client representatives participate in the focus group. Most focus groups are conducted on behalf of a business so this means having someone from that business participate either openly or in secret. This can be very insightful for the client, especially if he or she is there incognito. Plus it allows them to direct discussion to areas that are particularly important.
- **Mini focus groups** – groups are composed of 4 or 5 people rather than the more usual 8 to 12. This is particularly useful if a more intimate, detailed approach is called for.

Why does it matter?

Focus groups matter because they provide a platform to ask people about their opinions, beliefs, thoughts and attitudes around a particular topic, problem, product or service.

While engaged in lively discussion, members reveal feelings, through verbal and non-verbal communication, that a simple questionnaire may be unable to capture.

Focus groups are frequently used in product development and marketing so that a company can gauge how the product will be received and what tweaks they may need to make prior to release.

How can I use it in practice?

The dynamic nature of open-ended questions means that focus groups are ideal for really unpicking how someone thinks and feels about something. And perhaps more importantly the interaction with others creates greater dialogue and discussion than a qualitative survey which usually provides more insight.

Pretence, political correctness and outright lying by group members can undermine the value of focus groups. Also, some participants may have difficulty articulating their true feelings.

Focus groups usually last between 90 minutes to 2 hours and group members will answer five or six questions during that time. This is ideal if you need access to information or opinion quickly.

How do I get started?

You need to be clear about what you are trying to find out and devise a specific set of questions which, when answered, will provide you with the information you need.

Decide what areas you want to discuss and create some questions that can open the discussion. Obviously you are dealing with individuals in a group setting which means that the questions you prepare may only act as a starting point. You will usually get more detail and more insight if you allow the people in the focus group free rein to discuss the items on the agenda.

That said, there needs to be a facilitator to make sure that the right questions are being answered and to move people onto new topics or to get them back on track if they start to stray off the point.

Possible data sources

The data is collected by the moderator who will make detailed notes and flip chart notes.

Plus the focus groups are often video recorded or audio recorded which can provide more data for analysis through partial or full transcription together with text (Chapter 8) or voice analytics (Chapter 12) and sentiment analysis (Chapter 9).

The facilitator may also get participants to complete questionnaires which would also provide additional data (see Chapters 19 and 20).

How difficult or costly is it to collect?

Focus groups are relatively easy to organise and facilitate in that you are only ever involving small groups of people and gathering their information and insights into a particular topic.

As a result they are also much less expensive than other data capture techniques. However, if focus groups are run in multiple locations across a market, in order to gather variations in options across the market, then the costs can begin to spiral.

Practical example

If you wanted to know more about what your employees thought about a change to the business or were seeking to understand more about employee attitudes so you could positively influence or enhance the culture then focus groups could prove useful.

In this instance you could invite a range of different employees across different divisions and departments as well as different levels of seniority. Often this type of discussion across areas of levels of management would never occur naturally and it can yield some surprising insights for a business seeking to engage its workforce.

Tips and traps

Considering why you are considering running a focus group and therefore what information you are seeking to identify or uncover and use the best type of focus group to best facilitate that outcome. If, for example, you want to know more about what customers think about your products, running the occasional client participation focus group could yield additional insights because it would allow you to ask a lot of additional questions in the guise of a customer and see what other customers thought about it. Often people are less guarded when they think they are being asked a question by someone just like them. Plus, while engaged in lively discussion, members reveal feelings through verbal and non-verbal communication that a simple questionnaire may be unable to capture. Pretence, political correctness and outright lying by group members can undermine the value of focus groups. Also, some participants may have difficulty articulating their true feelings but skilled facilitation can overcome most of these traditional traps.

Further reading and references

To learn more about conducting focus groups see for example:

- Krueger, R.A. and Casey, M.A. (2014) *Focus Groups: A Practical Guide for Applied Research*, 5th edition, London: SAGE Publications
- Kamberelis, G. and Dimitriadis, G. (2013) *Focus Groups: From Structured Interviews to Collective Conversations*, 1st edition, Abingdon: Routledge
- http://www.hse.gov.uk/stress/standards/pdfs/focusgroups.pdf
- http://www.strath.ac.uk/aer/materials/3datacollection/unit1/focusgroups/
- http://web.stanford.edu/group/ncpi/unspecified/student_assess_toolkit/focusGroups.html
- http://ntweb.deltastate.edu/abarton/OldCourses/SOC474SP06/SOC474Pages/Green,%20Focus%20Grp%20Analysis.pdf
- http://www.utexas.edu/academic/ctl/assessment/iar/research/report/focus-analyze.php

Interviews

22

What is it?

An interview is a one-to-one or one-to-many conversation where the interviewer will ask questions in order to understand a topic or gather more information from the person or people being interviewed.

There are a number of different types of interview:

- **Informal, conversational interview** – no pre-prepared questions are asked so as to maintain an open and fluid conversation. The interview direction will depend on the answers as the interviewer and interviewee 'goes with the flow'.

- **General interview guide approach** – pre-set areas for discussion are agreed to ensure that the same general areas are discussed for every interview. This offers more structure than the informal approach, which also allows the interview to adapt if necessary.

- **Standardised open-ended interview** – the same pre-set open-ended questions are asked to everyone being interviewed. For example, job interviews tend to follow this approach so that every candidate is asked the same questions. This is fairer, faster and makes comparison and analysis easier.

- **Closed, fixed-response interview** – the same questions are asked to everyone being interviewed and each person must respond to the question from the same set of alternative answers.

Why does it matter?

Interviews matter because they allow for the collection of much richer data regarding a topic. Interviews tend to be much more intimate and so people can tell you more than they might expect to tell you or want to tell you.

The benefits of using interviews to gather data is the ability to dig behind the initial answers to really get to the nuggets of information or useful insights. Interviewing someone allows you to paint a much more vivid picture of what happened in a specific event or situation and allows you to hear the different individual perspectives on that event. Because the interview is usually in person in an intimate setting it is also possible for the interviewer to pick up on social cues such as voice tonality and body language which can help direct the discussion. This intimacy and verbal, and non-verbal, data download can help shed light on otherwise hidden connections between people, emotions, thoughts, events, behaviour and situations, which few other forms of data collection allows.

How can I use it in practice?

Interviews can be used in practice when you want to understand the meaning of central themes or to understand what the person being interviewed really thinks about certain topics.

Questionnaires can be quite impersonal and formulated, whereas if you get people talking they can often reveal far more about what is driving their behaviour or their actions. It is this meaning data that can be particularly useful.

In order for them to yield value, however, you need to know what it is you want to know and why. Make sure you are very clear about why you are conducting the interviews.

How do I get started?

Being able to interview others effectively requires skill. Being able to listen is crucial as is tact and sensitivity. If you don't naturally have those skills then either consider training or seek to outsource the interviews to someone who is skilled in this area.

The effectiveness of this data collection approach will also depend on who is interviewed. Take some time to consider what types of people you want to interview and why.

If you are a novice interviewer, and even if you are not, it is always wise to record the interviews so that you can go over them after the event and perhaps pick up additional insights. You can choose to record your interview using audio or video, although audio can be more discrete and tends not to intimidate the interviewee as much as video.

Possible data sources

Possible data sources include written notes from the interviewer. That said, the interviewer's primary role is to direct and manage the interview, so it's always preferable to record the interview to ensure all data is captured.

The recordings, either video or audio, can then be partially or completely transcribed for further analysis including text analytics (Chapter 8), voice analytics (Chapter 12) and sentiment analysis (Chapter 9).

How difficult or costly is it to collect?

Interviews are not difficult to organise but depending on how many interviews you plan to conduct they can be quite expensive. In order to ensure you gather all the information you can you will need to record them and potentially transcribe the recordings, which can soon mount up.

Practical example

Interviews are often used as the data collection methods when people leave an organisation. Known as 'exit interviews' these are designed to discover what caused the individual to leave to assess whether it's a one-off or something that the company could change to reduce staff turnover.

Obviously if a person is leaving a business then they can be quite hostile but an impartial interviewer can often extract reasons for the departure that may not be known without the exit interview.

Exit interviews allow for a thorough download of what went right and what went wrong with the role so that changes can be made to improve the experience for employees and potentially reduce costly absenteeism and turnover.

Tips and traps

As always, it is important to be really clear on the information you are seeking to identify and work out ahead of time what questions you are trying to answer.

Ultimately the quality of the data will depend on the skill of the interviewer and the quality of those being interviewed. Don't simply assume that anyone can run the interviews. Plus, it is important to account for interviewer bias. Everyone goes into an interview situation with their own unique set of behaviours, beliefs and values which can inadvertently skew the results.

Further reading and references

To understand more about conducting interviews see for example:

- Brinkmann, S. and Kvale, S. (2014) *InterViews: Learning the Craft of Qualitative Research Interviewing*, 3rd edition, London: SAGE Publications
- Seidman, I. (2012) Interviewing as Qualitative Research: A Guide for Researchers in Education and the Social Sciences, 4th edition, New York: Teachers College Press

- http://www.socialresearchmethods.net/kb/intrview.php
- http://www.kent.ac.uk/careers/intervw.htm
- http://www.edu.plymouth.ac.uk/resined/interviews/inthome.htm
- http://www.academia.edu/746649/Methods_of_data_collection_in_
  qualitative_research_interviews_and_focus_groups
- http://www.qualitative-research.net/index.php/fqs/article/view/175/391

Ethnography

23

What is it?

Ethnography is the study of people in a group setting. The term is derived from the Greek *ethnos* and *grapho*, meaning 'folk, people, nation' and 'I write', respectively. Ethnography is therefore the observation and documentation of the social behaviours, interactions and perceptions that occur within certain groups or cultures.

The roots of ethnography as a data collection practice can be traced back to anthropological studies of small, rural, often remote societies that were undertaken in the early 1900s. More recently it has been successfully applied to a variety of other group settings such as urban or corporate behaviour.

There are ethical issues around ethnography around whether the study should be declared or undeclared. While it is believed that more accurate information is gathered if the study is undeclared there are ethical issues associated with this approach. For instance, in one well-known example several researchers joined a cult that believed the world was going to end posing as true believers, but their real interest lay in understanding how people respond when something they deeply believe to be true turns out to be false. Of course this raises ethical issues, but they simply would not have been able to study the group accurately if they had declared their true intentions.

Why does it matter?

Ethnography matters because it provides rich, broad and far-reaching insights into people's opinions, views, beliefs, values and behaviour within a particular setting or environment.

Rather than bringing people in for interview or asking them questions via questionnaire ethnography allows the researcher to witness what's actually happening in the group as the group goes about its normal daily life. This can often yield far more information and more accurate information. Rather than asking what someone would or might do in a certain situation the researcher witnesses what the various people actually do in that situation. As such, it's more reliable. The aim of ethnography is to 'get inside' the group to see how it operates and really sees the world.

How can I use it in practice?

Ethnography could best be used in a business setting to observe a group or team working or in an environment where you are keen to figure out how people are interacting with each other. Perhaps you are keen to see how various departments work from the inside and assess the culture of the business or division.

Another way it can be applied is in a customer setting to better understand your target customer groups and their behaviours and belief patterns.

How do I get started?

First you need to decide what group you are going to study and in what setting. The idea is that the researcher infiltrates or lives alongside the group as they go about their normal daily activities.

Once the group has been identified and the purpose clarified, it is important for the researcher to win the cooperation of the 'gatekeeper' and key stakeholders in the group.

Traditionally, the ethnographer selects knowledgeable informants or stakeholders who know the activities of the group well. These individuals are then asked to identify other stakeholders who represent the group. This sampling process can often reveal common cultural denominators connected to the topic being studied. This type of research is data collection up close and personal, which means that getting gatekeepers and key stakeholders on board is very important. Without their agreement and cooperation it will be very difficult to gather the information needed to ensure the study is successful.

Developing trust and rapport with the group members being observed is an important part of ethnography studies and it is important to remain open and flexible so that the research can unfold as the events unfold.

Possible data sources

This type of research and data gathering is highly observational, although it may include interviews (Chapter 22), surveys (Chapters 19 and 20), content analysis, video and voice analysis (Chapters 11 and 12) and detailed 'field' notes.

Meticulous note taking is essential for ethnography and there are usually four types of data being collected:

- hasty note taking made as soon as possible after fieldwork or ideally during fieldwork;
- recording snippets of conversations;

- routine and significant incidents that occur during the study;
- detailed notes of what happened, when and how others reacted that are written up after fieldwork. These are usually completed after the ethnographer is out of the group setting.

Audio or video interviews or recorded interactions may be transcribed. This can help the researcher to take copious field notes for text analysis (Chapter 8) or sentiment analysis (Chapter 9).

How difficult or costly is it to collect?

Ethnography is not a structured research method so data collection is not necessarily simple or straightforward. It can also be quite time-consuming so it's certainly not the most cost-effective type of analytics that you could consider.

Practical example

Ethnography can provide clues to trends in human society; the identification of unmet needs that if identified early enough can be very useful and profitable for business.

Advertising agencies often use ethnography to ensure that ads are effectively targeted at a desirable population.

Alternatively, product design departments can also use ethnography to assess how a new product is actually used in the real world and how it could be improved. This is particularly valuable at prototype stage when there is a need to understand real end-user needs, or to understand the constraints of using a new product or service by a particular audience.

Tips and traps

Take care not to indicate a desired outcome from the observation as people tend to conform to what's expected of them. Encourage a natural 'fly on the wall' perspective so that participants or those being observed don't feel threatened or on display.

Don't be tempted to choose a small sample size as this can easily skew the results. The purpose of ethnography is to describe patterns of behaviour that could help predict the future or improve a product or service to fit that behaviour.

Further reading and references

To learn more about ethnography and how it could help your business see for example:

- Fetterman, D.M. (2009) *Ethnography: Step-by-Step*, 3rd edition, London: SAGE Publications

- http://www.strath.ac.uk/aer/materials/2designstrategiesineducationalresear ch/unit3/ethnography/
- http://www.cardiff.ac.uk/socsi/research/researchgroups/ethnographyculture/ index.html
- http://www.wisegeek.com/what-is-ethnography.htm
- https://www.gov.uk/service-manual/user-centred-design/user-research/ ethnographic-research.html
- http://smallbusiness.chron.com/ethnographic-research-marketing-25205 .html

Text capture

What is it?

If you want to run any type of text-based analytics then clearly you need text to analyse. In most businesses there is already a vast amount of text data available that could be analysed although it will need to be captured in a form that can then be used. This always means electronically and where the text is datafied rather than just digitised.

If you were to scan a text document, you have effectively created an electronic image of the document which means the document is digitised as a soft copy but it is not datafied. You couldn't search that scanned document for a phrase or run any analysis on the text because each word is not stored separately as text, rather it is stored as a single image file. This means that while a human being may be able to open that electronic copy of the document and read it, a machine can't. If you want to analyse text the text must be datafied.

Why does it matter?

Text capture matters because advances in analytics mean that there are now many more insights that can be drawn from text than ever before. These insights relate to what the text actually says but also go way beyond the actual words and phrases used to the meaning, emotion and sentiment behind the words.

Plus, text already exists in huge quantities inside most businesses. Often it is untouched and yet with a little effort can yield many commercially relevant insights that can improve performance and profitability.

How can I use it in practice?

There are many ways to capture text data. If the volume of text you want to analyse is quite small then you could re-type physical documents to create a datafied electronic form, but this is labour-intensive and therefore costly.

There are a number of text recognition and text capture tools that convert physical documents to electronic datafied documents. These include:

- **Optical character recognition (OCR)** – this technology will capture machine produced characters on a form or a page. OCR systems can recognise multiple fonts as well as typewriter and computer-printed characters. As most text is machine generated via a computer, tablet or smartphone, OCR systems can help in the efficient capture of text for analysis.

- **Intelligent character recognition (ICR)** – this technology will translate hand-printed and written text. This is more sophisticated because it has to account for variations in handwriting.

- **Barcode recognition** – a lot of meta-data is often stored on barcodes on documents such as delivery notes, or membership and application forms, which can then be captured and used for analytic purposes.

- **Intelligent document recognition (IDR)** – these tools can capture 'rule based' text such as postcodes, logos, key words. They also learn as they go along so can become increasingly useful for text capture the more they are used. These types of tools are often used for mail sorting.

We all know that what someone says in text is not always what they mean and text analytics (Chapter 8) and sentiment analysis (Chapter 9) can help to understand customers, shareholders, employees and competitors much more accurately, which can ensure better decision making.

How do I get started?

First you need to know what you are trying to figure out, what questions you are seeking to find answers to and what text data could potentially help you to answer those questions.

If possible, it makes sense to use text data you already have or have easy access to by using some of the text capture tools readily available on the market.

Of course there are also other valuable sources of data that can quite easily be converted into text such as employee performance reviews or customer service conversations. If you already have a customer services department where the calls are being recorded then voice recognition or speech-to-text software could be used on those voice recordings to create an endless stream of relevant, up-to-date text for ongoing customer analysis.

Depending on what key questions you want to know the answers to, you can also trigger text creation from your customers or stakeholder group by asking for feedback. For example, after an online order process the customer could be asked to leave feedback about how easy the process was.

Possible data sources

There are many possible text data sources including:

- corporate documents such as letters, contract agreements and correspondence;
- email;
- customer communication;
- social media posts;
- invoices;
- fax;
- recorded conversations, i.e. customer service.

How difficult or costly is it to collect?

There is already an abundance of text data in most businesses that can inexpensively be used for analysis. The cost will usually accumulate when you need to convert hard copies or scanned documents to digitised and datafied files. That said, there are a growing number of inexpensive tools to help with that process.

In addition, voice recognition software and speech-to-text software is very affordable and surprisingly accurate and effective.

Practical example

A call centre generates a vast amount of data around what customers are buying, what they like, don't like, what annoys them and how effective the sales and customer service staff are at their job. Traditionally, a lot of that data was lost because, even if the interactions were recorded, they were only recorded for security and training purposes or for proof of conversation should a problem arise.

Now all that voice data can be collected and converted to text without human involvement, which provides a treasure trove of data for ongoing assessment. Not only can this data improve customer service but it can identify product gaps in the market or innovations that would or could improve the product or service.

Tips and traps

Be really clear about what you are hoping to discover from the text you collect. Often when companies first consider the sheer volume of text data they have they can become overwhelmed and think they need to convert everything to a digitised and datafied form. Focus on the most recent data only. Unless there is a very good reason for going back 5 or 10 years, the data will be out of date anyway – so forget the past and where possible gather real-time text data for analysis.

When we think of text we often think of a physical hard copy of a letter or contract, but often the text is already in digital form when it is sent to you such as customer emails or PDF invoices. Don't feel you have to print that out and then convert to datafied text. This is an unnecessary, time-consuming and potentially costly course of action.

Further reading and references

To find out more about text capture see for example:

- http://processflows.co.uk/data-capture/methods-of-data-capture/

Image capture

What is it?

If you want to run analytics on images then you need to have the images to analyse. This process is therefore the dedicated collection of useful images for that purpose.

With the increase of social media platforms and smartphones there is now an abundance of images that could potentially be useful for analysis.

Why does it matter?

Image data matters because a picture paints a thousand words and that is still true. There is a huge amount of information that can be gleaned from a photograph or image above and beyond what is contained in the image. For example, photographs have GPS-based meta-data that will tell you when the photograph was taken as well as where the photograph was taken.

How can I use it in practice?

Image data can be very useful in manufacturing and improving customer service. If a part is faulty, for example, a picture of the fault can often help the manufacturing team to understand the problem better. If all faults are always recorded with a photograph of the problem then it's more likely that consistently faulty parts can be identified and improved.

Insurance companies often now ask for photographs of the incident or damage that is initiating an insurance claim. In addition, when a customer is unhappy with a product or service they can be asked to send a photograph of the fault to fast track the return process.

Crime prevention has been using image capture data for a long time, taking multiple pictures of a crime scene to record as much data as possible.

Once you have the image data you can apply image and video analytics (Chapters 10 and 11) and sentiment analysis (Chapter 9).

How do I get started?

The best place to start when gathering image data is to identify what image data you already have and whether it's going to be useful. Also, as always be very clear about what questions you want your image data to answer.

Consider how images and photographs could help you to improve your products, services and customer service. This is especially true now as so many people have smartphones and are constantly walking around with a camera in their pocket. Asking for a customer or employee to take a photograph of a fault or incident is no longer an imposition. If a photograph will be useful ask for it.

Also, if you have CCTV footage for security purposes this can be easily converted to image data.

Possible data sources

There are many possible image data sources including:

- photographs;
- graphics;
- online images;
- video footage;
- CCTV footage.

How difficult or costly is it to collect?

Whether you already have access to image data or not, most people have constant access to a good-quality camera via their smartphone so if you think image data could help you to improve your products or services then ask your customers for photographs.

You could run online competitions or ask via feedback areas on your website so customers can upload photographs of faults or new and novel ways that they use your product. This type of insight could lead to new product developments and improvements.

Practical example

The king of image analytics is probably Facebook! Billions of people use Facebook and happily upload 350 million images every day![1] To say they have a lot of image

---

[1]IACP Centre for Social Media Fun Facts http://www.iacpsocialmedia.org/Resources/FunFacts.aspx

data would be a staggering understatement – all provided for free by us. The result is a massive image library which has allowed Facebook researchers to create their DeepFace pattern recognition system capable of achieving near-human face recognition accuracy. The software automatically converts the topography of each face in the image gallery into a unique mathematical code, called a faceprint. This faceprint can then be used to identify an individual from other photographs online, subsequent photos uploaded to social media sites or CCTV footage.

Using the photographs users willingly upload, Facebook is able to create a 3D image of their face and then scan the rest of the internet to find other pictures of those people to see where else they appear and who else they might know. So, for example, Facebook can and are matching your uploaded Facebook images to your corporate website, online dating profile or find you in news articles or blog posts. This way companies are able to triangulate the data they have on you and find out even more. There will come a time in the not-too-distant future when Facebook will be able to monitor your photographs and notice if you have put on weight. That data could then be sold on to weight-loss companies for targeted advertising.

Tips and traps

Encourage your customers and employees to record images and send in photographs of your products and services in use. Build up a database of images that can then be analysed to discover trends. For example, you may discover that while one particular product is sold in a particular store it is being used at a different location, which could indicate a potential new market.

Remember the time when photographs only existed in physical form? While they may be useful for retro marketing or illustrate how your products have changed over the years don't get too hung up on converting all your old physical images into digital form – unless there is a specific reason for it.

Further reading and references

To find out more about image capture see for example:

- Baughman, A., Gao, J. and Pan, J.-Y. (eds) (2015) *Multimedia Data Mining and Analytics: Disruptive Innovation Hardcover*, New York: Springer
- Shan, C., Porikli, F., Xiang, T. and Gong, S. (eds) (2012) *Video Analytics for Business Intelligence*, New York: Springer
- Daoudi, M., Srivastava, A. and Veltkamp, R. (2013) *3D Face Modeling, Analysis and Recognition*, Hoboken, NJ: Wiley

26

Sensor data

What is it?

A sensor is a device, usually electronic, that takes a physical quality such as temperature or light, measures it and converts it into information or data that can then be analysed for insights.

Sensors have been around for a long time but their range and application has increased exponentially resulting in the Internet of Things (IoT) – where more and more objects are being manufactured with embedded sensors which gather data and allows those objects to communicate with each other. You can already buy carpet with inbuilt sensors that can tell when someone walks on it! This is being used by people concerned about an elderly relative to make sure they are safe and moving about. With the Internet of Things the sensors in the carpet could potentially communicate with sensors in the coffee machine so that as soon as someone gets out of bed in the morning and stands on the carpet this data triggers the coffee machine to turn on so that there is a hot cup of coffee waiting for you after you've taken your morning shower.

Advances in smart, sensor-based technology and connectivity promise to create new business models, improve business processes and performance while also reducing cost and potentially risk.

Why does it matter?

Sensors matter because they allow us to collect and analyse important data that can be used to deliver a whole range of benefits from improving performance to warning about a fault to measuring activity or safety.

There are only so many hours in the day and no one person or even a team of people can be expected to measure and monitor everything. Sensors can provide the data without any human involvement, freeing up human beings to do work that only human beings can do.

How can I use it in practice?

The application of sensors is literally endless. Most modern products are created with sensors. A smartphone, for example, is smart because of its sensors. A GPS (Global Positioning System) sensor identifies where we are using the GPS satellite navigation system and so long as we are with our phone it can pinpoint our location within a few metres. An accelerometer sensor detects acceleration or how quickly the phone is moving. It's this technology that allows us to take better photos with our smartphones because it triggers the shutter when the camera is stationary or stable. A gyroscope sensor is used to maintain orientation and is used to rotate the screen. It is this sensor that is often utilised in gaming apps where you have to tilt the screen to direct the character or steer a racing car. A proximity sensor senses how close we are to other objects or locations – it is this type of sensor that is built into modern cars to help us to parallel park. Ambient sensors are the ones that detect changes in the ambiance or atmosphere, so it is this sensor that adjusts the backlight on our phone or saves power when it's not being actively used. And finally, an NFC sensor is one of the latest communication protocols being utilised in smartphones. It is these NFC sensors that, when enabled, allow us to transfer funds just by bumping phones or waving our phone close to an appropriate payment machine.

There are also sensors in the natural environment – in the oceans for measuring the health, temperature and changes of the oceans in real time. Also, in Japan there are sensors in the soil to collect data on the soil's health. That data can then be combined with weather data to help farmers optimise yield, including how much and when to put fertiliser on the crop.

Sensors can be applied to just about anything and can be used to measure just about anything so they could be extremely useful in gathering data that can then help your decision making.

How do I get started?

How you get started will depend on what you are trying to measure. Consider the possible data sources below and apply that to your business. Would you like to know how your customers move around your store for example – that could be achieved by measuring movement via some well-positioned sensors.

Perhaps you would like to save on your energy costs in your factory or office building – this could be achieved by sensors that detect movement or temperature so that if there is no one in a location the lights will be turned off automatically.

Suffice to say, the data gathering and application of sensor data is enormous.

Possible data sources

There are many different types of sensors which measure a variety of variables including:

- Temperature – capable of detecting whether something gets hotter or colder. This could be very useful for triggering intervention and safety issues.

- Light – capable of detecting changes in light from light to dark. This could be useful in minimising energy usage.
- Pressure – capable of measuring if a component is under pressure or too much pressure.
- Moisture – capable of measuring if something such as a machine part or an environment is becoming too dry or too damp. This could be useful if a product needs to be created in a particular environment or operates most effectively within a certain tolerance.
- Level – capable of detecting the level of something such as the water level in an engine. This could be useful for ensuring a machine runs optimally.
- Movement – capable of detecting movement. Again this could be useful within an engine or part to make sure the movement is within a normal range so as to minimise breakdown and wear and tear.
- Proximity – capable of detecting if something is close or too close. This can be useful where objects need to be kept away from each other such as large machinery or plant equipment.

How difficult or costly is it to collect?

Sensors come in a wide variety of forms and function; from the very small and dis-crete to the most complex and elaborate equipment. Technological innovation is, however, lowering the size and cost all the time.

Even now using sensors to gather data is a very cost-effective method because it is done automatically without human involvement and yields a lot of consistent and accurate data.

Practical example

I worked with a small fashion retail company that had no data other than their traditional sales data. They wanted to increase sales but didn't really know where to start. They didn't know how successful their window display was or how many people came into the shop, or how many then converted to a sale. So we installed a small, discrete sensor into the shop windows that tracked mobile phone signals as people walked past the shop. The sensors would also measure how many people stopped to look at the window and for how long, and how many people then walked into the store – sales data would record who actually bought something.

By combining the data from inexpensive, readily available sensors placed in the window with transaction data we were able to measure conversion ratio, and test window displays and various offers to see which ones increased sales. By using sensor data strategically they increased revenue and also reduced costs signifi-cantly. Prior to opening the stores the retailer engaged a market research firm to assess the best location for each one. The sensor data proved that the footfall reported by the market research company was wrong and the passing traffic was insufficient to justify keeping one of the stores open. It was then closed, freeing up resources to focus on the stores that were making money.

Tips and traps

As with any data, it is important to collect the relevant and most meaningful data to help you answer your business questions. Because we are now surrounded by sensors, the biggest issue with sensor data is that it can be so easily generated in large quantities that we often collect too much data instead of the right data.

Another concern is privacy. Many people get increasingly concerned with the amount of data that is generated by sensors and machines that surround them. My recommendation is to be very open and make people aware of the sensors, what data they are collecting and how that data will be used.

Further reading and references

To find out more about sensor data and how it could benefit your business see for example:

- Kelly, J. E. and Hamm, S. (2013) *Smart Machines: IBM's Watson and the Era of Cognitive Computing*, New York: Columbia Business School Publishing

- Scoble, R. and Israel, S. (2013) *Age of Context: Mobile, Sensors, Data and the Future of Privacy*, 1st edition, CreateSpace Independent Publishing Platform

- Kellmereit, D. and Obodovski, D. (2013) *The Silent Intelligence: The Internet of Things*, 1st edition, DND Ventures LLC

- Aggarwal, C. (ed) (2013) *Managing and Mining Sensor Data*, New York: Springer

- http://www.ehow.com/about_4621381_different-types-sensors.html

- http://electronics.howstuffworks.com/gadgets/high-tech-gadgets/rfid.htm

27 Machine data capture

What is it?

Machine data capture is basically sensors that are embedded into machines. This is therefore particularly useful for manufacturers or businesses that use machines in the creation of their product.

Data captured from machines allows a manufacturer to monitor and measure the health and efficiency of machines and allows them to manage operations more effectively and minimise down time. Where sensors are embedded into products these sensors can also provide the owner and/or manufacturer with important information that can improve the product over time.

Why does it matter?

Machine data capture matters because often large manufacturers rely on machine efficiency and minimising down times in order to meet their productivity targets. Traditionally, equipment, often expensive important equipment, is put on a time-based maintenance and parts replacement schedule. Machines are therefore taken offline several times a year, checked over by a mechanic and new parts installed on a regular basis 'just in case'. Often those parts are expensive as is having the machine offline for several days. Machine data capture means that sensors can be embedded into the machines to measure a wide variety of variables. The data is then fed back to computers that monitor the machine performance and alert a human being should a part need to be replaced or the machine is running less than optimally. This real-time monitoring of machine data can create significant savings and increase output.

How can I use it in practice?

Whether you use machines in your manufacturing process or are creating machines or devices for sale, embedded sensors can monitor performance and provide extremely valuable information on when best to service or repair the machines.

Embedded sensors inside the machines, connected to particular parts or processes, can monitor efficiency and indicate when there is cause for concern or if a part is not performing properly. This can allow maintenance to fix the problem before the machine actually breaks down which can minimise machine down time and unnecessary servicing.

If you create equipment, machines or devices as your product, embedding sensors can also be a source of competitive advantage. If your product provides your buyer with information that can make their life easier, better or safer over and above the purpose of the product then that product will be viewed more favourably than your competitors.

For example, it is now possible to buy nappies with embedded sensors that send a message to the parent when the child needs changing. Obviously most good parents will already know when their child needs changing but these sensors also monitor the contents of the nappy for abnormalities and alert the parent of any potential health issues.

How do I get started?

As machine data capture is basically a sub-set of sensor data collection, you can either install sensors into machines and equipment or you can leverage sensors that are already inbuilt into machines that you purchase. In many cases it simply means connecting the machines to your IT system to collect and analyse the data. With many modern machines they already have wireless connectivity via Wi-Fi or Bluetooth connections and often come with software or apps to monitor and analyse the data, which makes the whole process a lot easier.

Possible data sources

Possible data sources are any machines with inbuilt sensors or any Internet of Things device that allows you to collect data. These sensors can effectively measure anything that changes including:

- temperature;
- light;
- pressure;
- humidity;
- level;
- movement;
- proximity;
- and much more.

How difficult or costly is it to collect?

How difficult and costly machine data capture is will depend on the age of the machines you are seeking to measure, the cost and availability of the sensors that will measure what you have identified and whether it's viable to add sensors.

Most modern equipment already has sensors built in so equipment replacement over time will usually take care of sensor data. If, however, you have older pre-sensor equipment you may need to investigate how to take advantage of the mountains of valuable data they can yield. That said, many sensors are very affordable and offer significant value for money.

Practical example

As well as providing performance information, machine capture data may end up changing your business model.

For example, Rolls-Royce manufactures nearly half the world's passenger jet engines and those engines are full of embedded sensors. These sensors monitor performance in real time by measuring some 40 parameters 40 times per second including temperatures, pressures and turbine speeds. All the data is then stored in on-board computers and is simultaneously streamed via satellite back to Rolls-Royce HQ in Derby, England. There, computers then sift through the data to look for anomalies. If any are found they are immediately flagged and a human being will check the results and if necessary telephone the airline and work out what needs to be done – often before the issue escalates into an actual problem.

These sensors therefore allow for dynamic maintenance based on actual engine-by-engine performance rather than some automatic rota system based on time alone. Instead of pulling an expensive piece of equipment out of service every three or six months, these sensors allow the airlines to maintain their fleet much more cost-effectively, and more importantly these sensors make the planes much safer.[1]

And this innovation has changed Rolls-Royce's business model. The company used to just make the engines, but now they monitor the engines too using thousands of sensors positioned throughout the engines. These sensors continuously monitor the performance of more than 3,700 jet engines worldwide to identify issues before they arise. As a result Rolls-Royce have moved their business model from solely manufacturing to the creation of recurring ongoing revenue streams over and above their manufacturing business. Now Rolls-Royce sells the engines and offers to monitor them, charging customers based on engine usage time, and repairs and replaces parts if there is a problem. So the client effectively buys a dynamic servicing option and this servicing now accounts for a massive 70 per cent of the civil-aircraft engine division's annual revenue.[2]

---

[1] BBC 2 *Bang Goes the Theory* Series 8 'Big Data' (March 2014)

[2] Mayer-Schönberger, V. and Cukier, K. (2013) *Big Data: A revolution that will transform how we live, work and think*, London: John Murray Publishers

Tips and traps

When machines you purchase come with ready-made apps and inbuilt data capture this makes it easy but can also lead to information overload. A modern Airbus has over 10,000 sensors in a single wing alone. Our cars are full of sensors and so are most machines we buy. When they then come with their own apps it is sometimes difficult to identify the data that is really relevant to your business. Instead of using many different proprietary apps and reporting software applications it is often better to pull the relevant data in your own analytics and reporting systems so that you only capture, analyse and report the information that matters.

Further reading and references

For more information about machine data capture see for example:

- Kelly, J.E. and Hamm, S. (2013) *Smart Machines: IBM's Watson and the Era of Cognitive Computing*, New York: Columbia Business School Publishing
- http://dbmsmusings.blogspot.co.uk/2010/12/machine-vs-human-generated-data.html
- http://www.dbms2.com/2010/04/08/machine-generated-data-example/

[PART THREE]

Financial analytics

Predictive sales analytics

28

What is it?

Predictive sales analytics is the process of figuring out how successful your sales forecast is and how to improve your sales predictions in the future.

Many companies now employ an analytics group that is responsible for data mining (Chapter 6) and analysis. This data mining activity looks for trends and relationships in the sales data which could help sales and marketing make more accurate sales predictions.

Alternatively, for smaller companies this type of analytics may be outsourced to a specialist data mining company that will determine future sales.

Why does it matter?

Sales revenue is the lifeblood of any business so knowing how much you can expect to receive has important tactical and strategic implications.

The ability to accurately predict sales matters because it provides valuable information for inventory management, staffing and cash flow management. Clearly, if you can accurately predict sales volume in the future, you can make or source only the products you need and manage inventory more efficiently so as to meet demand but not hold too much stock at any one time. Sales forecasts can also help you to ensure you have enough staff to handle the workload and ensure the best possible customer service. Sales revenue also drives cash flow, which is essential for any business. Knowing what to expect and when can help to make sure the business makes provisions to manage the slower periods as well as the busy periods.

Predictive sales analytics can also be used to secure funding and provide valuable customer data. If you are looking to secure a loan or financing from a third party for equipment or expansion you will need to demonstrate revenue and potential future revenue to prove your ability to repay the loan. Sales analytics can provide that data which can help facilitate the loan's approval. Plus, this data can help you and the sales people to predict trends or changes to buying patterns that could improve sales still further. When individual sales people have access to this data they know what customers bought in the past and when they bought, which can be used to initiate contact and re-sell or up-sell.

When do I use it?

Predictive sales analytics is an extremely useful tool for planning and peace of mind. If you know what to expect then you are in a much better position to manage the peaks and troughs of your business, without the fire-fighting and sleepless nights. As a result, it is wise to use predictive sales analytics all the time so that you can make better decisions in the business and scale up and down when needed.

For example, many businesses experience more and fewer sales at certain times of the year. If you know that year on year you make fewer sales in June and July then you can encourage staff to take a holiday during that time and not get too stressed that sales are dropping. Or you could take special measures to source and secure sales from other areas, or develop different products or services to dovetail into the slower periods.

What business questions is it helping me to answer?

Predictive sales analytics can help you to answer:

- How much product am I likely to sell in the next month/quarter/year?
- How are my sales fluctuating throughout the year?
- Are there any longer-term trends within the sales activity?
- How do my various product lines compare in sales throughout the year?

How do I use it?

There are several ways of predicting sales. The first is to use analytics on past sales data to see if you can identify any patterns or trends that can then help you to forecast future sales. Of course, past results are no guarantee of future results.

In order to apply predictive sales analytics there is certain sales data you will need to collect. First you will need to have detailed sales for each product broken down by month, number of returned sales broken down by month and any external factors, or one-off events that influenced sales.

You can also use predictive techniques like regression (Chapter 7) and/or correlation (Chapter 3) to identify aspects of your offer that are affecting sales so that you can predict sales in the future. Plus scenario analysis (Chapter 4), Monte Carlo simulations (Chapter 13) and neural networks (Chapter 17) are also used widely in this area.

For example, Shell have used scenario analysis for many years to create a number of different feasible scenarios and how those scenarios would impact oil price, potential demand and revenue over the next 20–25 years. Every month they will review the various scenarios to decide which are more likely to happen and what they can then do to mitigate their risks accordingly.

Depending on your business, scenario analysis can be incredibly useful to help you outline a number of different possible futures based on not only your own data but additional data sets such as economic forecasts, climate change data or data on the growing influence of pressure groups that could impact your business. That way you can be ready for the future – whatever that might be.

Practical example

Say you are considering acquiring an additional business or are considering expanding your operations. Both will require capital and the easiest way to expand or buy another business is to use your existing reserves. Not only do you need to predict sales to work out whether you will be able to fund your new venture internally, but even if you can't you will need to be able to predict future sales in order to secure funding.

Traditionally, we would look at past sales in order to do this so that we can then try to predict future sales. But this type of analytics starts to get really interesting when we also include some of the new data sets such as market trends, competitor data and even weather data.

For example, supermarkets will use weather data extensively to predict sales in the future and manage stock in the store. If the weather is due to be warm and sunny then they may promote their sausages and beef burgers and run in-store campaigns encouraging customers to enjoy the sun with a BBQ.

Initially this type of sales analytics started to help with stock control. Obviously stores only have so much space and there is no point using that space to offer a dizzying array of ice-cream in the winter! But now supermarkets are using this type of analytics further down the supply chain where they look at longer-term weather patterns to decide what suppliers to use in the first place.

Walmart use predictive sales analytics very successfully. They analyse buying patterns among similar types of customers and what competitors are charging in real-time as well as monitoring what's trending on social media. For example, they learned via social media that 'cake pops' were popular with consumers and the company was able to respond quickly and get them into stores.

Tips and traps

Predicting future sales is always helped by detailed and thorough sales data from the past so keep accurate records. Also, make sure you account for returned goods to ensure that your sales figures are not inflated.

Don't forget to take any unusual activity into account as this could easily skew the results and lead to inaccurate predictions.

Further reading and references

To find out more about predictive sales analytics see for example:

- McNelis, P.D. (2005) *Neural Networks in Finance: Gaining Predictive Edge in the Market*, 1st edition, Waltham, MA: Academic Press
- Siegel, E. (2013) *Predictive Analytics: The Power to Predict Who Will Click, Buy, Lie, or Die*, 1st edition, Hoboken, NJ: Wiley
- http://www.ehow.com/list_5986362_advantages-sales-forecasting.html
- http://www.businessbee.com/resources/sales/analytics-reporting/how-to-create-predictive-sales-reports-for-smarter-selling/
- http://practicalanalytics.wordpress.com/predictive-analytics-101/
- http://www.businessbee.com/resources/sales/how-to-use-predictive-analytics-tools-to-increase-your-sales/

Customer profitability analytics

29

What is it?

Customer profitability analytics is the process of identifying which of your customers are actually making you money. There is often an assumption in business that any customer is a good customer, but that is not always the case. Customer profitability usually falls within the Pareto principle or 80/20 rule.

In other words, there is likely to be 20 per cent of your customers that account for 80 per cent of your profit. Conversely there is also likely to be another 20 per cent of your customers that account for 80 per cent of your customer-related costs. Knowing which is which is important.

Why does it matter?

Customer profitability matters because if you can't differentiate between the customers that make you money and the customers that lose you money then you will treat all your customers the same and diminish your profitability.

When you can split your customers into groups you can tailor your marketing message and your level of service to each group. Customer profitability analytics provide you with a deep understanding of your customers' buying habits and the costs incurred in supplying the products they buy from you. This knowledge can help you to focus on the highest profit centres by really looking after those customers that are profitable and encourage the ones that cost you money to go to your competition.

When do I use it?

This metric is a valuable tool to be used all the time, but it is especially important during a difficult economic climate. Obviously if sales are down or costs are up and your business is not as profitable as it once was then this analytic tool can help you to understand why and take the necessary steps to get the business back on track.

By understanding the profitability of certain groups of customers you also have the opportunity to further analyse each group so you can understand any similarities within each group such as where they live, what they first purchased or where they were sourced from. For example, you may discover that your very best customers made their first purchase from a particular advertisement in a particular magazine and your least profitable customers were sourced from a direct mail campaign from a particular list. That knowledge can help direct your future marketing efforts so that you don't use that list again and consider more advertisements in the specific magazine.

What business questions is it helping me to answer?

Customer profitability analytics provides a rich analytic platform that allows for detailed assessment down to the particular deal or transaction and creates a degree of transparency that can generate really valuable insights. The business questions customer profitability analytics can help you answer include:

- How do my customers compare with each other in terms of profitability?
- How do marketing initiatives compare?
- How do sales people and regions compare?
- What percentages of our customers create most of our profit?

How do I use it?

Any organisation can use customer profitability analytics. Even not-for-profit organisations such as the NHS. Although such organisations don't have customers as such, they do have 'users' and while they are not seeking to make a profit they are definitely interested in making their budgets stretch as far as possible so they can help as many people as possible. For example, I did some work with the NHS using this type of analytics and they discovered that just 5 per cent of their patients were responsible for over 200 visits to accident and emergency. They were 'super-users' who clearly had separate issues beyond their 'day out in A&E'. So by highlighting these super-users they were able to seek different assistance to free up resources for others.

Customer profitability, whatever your definition of 'customer' is, can therefore help you to identify who is using your products and services. This not only helps you to focus on the more profitable customers but also identify ways to reduce costs.

This type of analytics is also very useful for broadband providers. Some customers – the super-users – may end up using so much in their unlimited deal that they become unprofitable. Often regression analysis (Chapter 7), correlation analysis (Chapter 3) or data mining (Chapter 6) is used to identify these different user/customer groups.

Practical example

Customer profitability analytics have been around since at least the early 1980s but they are still underused considering the gold mine of information they can yield.

Initially used in banking, this type of analytics allows you to measure the contribution each customer makes to overall profit as well as the key drivers of this profit. It is often considered to be a customer-level version of your P&L statement.

Say you provide electronic parts to large manufacturers, you may have 10,000 customers on your database going back many years. By using customer profitability analytics you can divide those 10,000 customers into percentage groups from the top 10 per cent to the bottom 10 per cent based on a variety of identifiers such as product, region, volume of sales, frequency of sales and customer service issues.

You may discover, for example, that one particular customer that your sales team love because they buy so frequently is actually a loss-making client because of the after-sales issues they always raise. So while this customer may look good on paper, deeper customer profitability analytics indicate that the same client always wastes a huge amount of time questioning and complaining about aspects of the product or delivery that renders them unprofitable.

Tips and traps

The biggest danger with customer profitability analytics is when you don't take a customer's full lifetime value. If you assess profitability of each customer across the product or service range you may miss their cumulative value. In many companies a customer who buys five different products is treated as five different customers rather than one customer who buys five products – this disconnect can flag up unprofitable customers where they are actually very profitable if seen in the full context of their buying behaviour.

It can also be easy to ignore or miss this analytic tool because profitability is the domain of the finance department so the picture and the detail of individual customer profitability can be lost. It's important that finance and customer service departments collaborate in this metric to extract additional valuable information that can direct marketing strategy and decision making.

Further reading and references

To learn more about customer profitability analytics see for example:

- Pfeifer, P.W. and Farris, P.E. (2009) *Customer Profitability*, Charlottesville, VA: Darden Business Publishing
- Reich, K.E. (1985) *Customer Profitability Analysis: A Tool for Improving Bank Profits*, 2nd edition, Chicago, IL: Probus Professional Publishing

- http://www.xlcubed.com/solutions/analytical-applications/20-customer-profitability-analytics
- https://www.accenture.com/bw-en/insight-determining-customer-profitability-banking-summary.aspx
- http://office.microsoft.com/en-us/templates/customer-profitability-analysis-TC001150736.aspx
- http://blog.visibleequity.com/customer-profitability-analytics/

Product profitability analytics

30

What is it?

Product profitability analytics is the process for discovering profitability by individual product. Most businesses know how profitable the business is but very few take the time to dig deeper into the individual profitability of each product or service they offer. As a result few businesses know which of their products are making money and which of their products are losing money.

In order for profitability analytics to be genuinely meaningful and commercially useful beyond revenue and gross margins, it is necessary to uncover hidden or specific profit and losses pertinent to the product range.

This is, however, much easier said than done. Many businesses have large, complex product lines and operationally it is often very difficult to separate costs across those product lines accurately. For example, methods used to allocate sales, marketing, advertising or customer service costs to each product can be much too arbitrary to yield any real value. Plus there are often multiple suppliers and changing raw material costs that can add to the confusion. But without an understanding of what products are profitable and which products are eating profit, poor strategic decisions are likely so it's always worth the effort.

Product profitability analytics helps businesses to uncover profitability insights across the product range so better decisions are made and profit is protected and grown over time.

Why does it matter?

It matters because businesses need to stay competitive and need to know where money is being made and lost. Product profitability analytics allows you to factor in the real costs associated with each product so that you can make adjustments which will positively impact profit.

If you discover that one product makes more profit than all the others then you may want to promote that product more heavily and invest in some research and development to find new more profitable products.

Alternatively if you discover that a product is making a loss then you can either make operational and production changes to bring the product into profit or drop the product from the line. Of course you would need to run additional analytics before you made any major decisions so you don't inadvertently damage profit.

For example, I worked with a supermarket that run product profitability on their product range and discovered that one of the washing up liquids that they stocked always lost money. In fact it was actually costing the supermarket money to stock the product. Looking at these results in isolation would indicate the supermarket should stop stocking the product. Luckily we were also doing a lot more analytics and also discovered that the people who bought that particularly washing up liquid happened to be their highest spenders. If they had removed that product from their shelves then it's highly likely they would have upset their most profitable customers who may have decided to go to a different supermarket to get that particular washing up liquid.

When do I use it?

You should consider using product profitability analytics when you start out in your business or whenever you change your product and service offering.

You should know what products are your winners, which are your loss leaders and which are your dogs at any given time. And you should make a point of reviewing that information strategically at least once a year.

There are usually significant costs involved in adding new products or services to your range so you want to be absolutely sure the ones you do add and keep are paying their way.

What business questions is it helping me to answer?

Product profitability analytics provides answers as to which products or services that you are offering make you money and which lose you money. The business questions product profitability analytics can help you answer include:

- Which products or services are profitable?
- Which products or services lose money?
- How do the products or services compare for profitability?

How do I use it?

In order to assess your product profitability you need to assess each product individually. So whereas the previous technique needed you to look at each customer individually, this time you need to assess the product. This will require a thorough assessment of costs.

This can be quite tricky because in every business there will be similar products or services that share production processes or cost bases. It can also be quite challenging to split and apportion costs where economies of scale have influenced costs. This technique will however only really be useful if you find a reliable and fair way to apportion costs to your various products.

Practical example

Take a mobile phone company for example. The business may produce and sell 20 different models of phone ranging from a basic smartphone with simple display through to state of the art smartphones that can do anything except make you a cup of tea.

If you were to look at revenue and the profit and loss statement you would see that the company is doing well. Smartphones are popular and the market is buoyant. Most people like to upgrade their new phone frequently so it's a strong ongoing market.

But the company doesn't know which of their phones are making the most money. They know which models sell best in terms of volume sold but have never assessed product profitability.

By implementing product profitability analytics the product manager is able to identify one product category that outperforms the others. In addition he identifies one category that is consistently losing money. Although one model sells well, it's high spec and that end of the market is crowded. Competing with big, established brands such as Apple is tough. Plus the technology is evolving rapidly, which means heavy ongoing R&D costs.

The simpler smartphone on the other hand is selling almost as well but has a far higher margin and less competition. Aimed at an older audience or starter smartphone this product has found a niche and is profiting from the niche.

In addition detailed product profitability analytics allows the product manager to see where the costs arise for each product the company sells and use that information to alter the production process or operations to minimise costs or drop the product from the range. These insights also impacted marketing and advertising as a new push toward the older customer helps to establish that model as a cash cow. Knowing more about what is happening with each product also allows the sales department to up-sell and cross-sell at appropriate times after the initial sale or sell additional products that were complimentary to the cash cow product. For example they developed a simple, easy-to-use tablet that complemented the phone and was an easy sell to existing happy customers.

Tips and traps

Don't automatically apportion operational costs equally across all products, or arbitrarily attribute costs without really digging deeply into how those costs should be allocated. Arbitrary and inaccurate cost allocation will skew the results and render the whole process pointless.

And watch out for loss leaders. Some products may lose you money but their purchase leads on to more profitable purchases. A customer may, for example, buy a cheap pay-as-you-go phone, but that may lead on to a contract phone and broadband purchase. Be sure you know the full story before taking action on a particular product.

Further reading and references

To understand more about product profitability analytics see for example:

- Haines, S. (2008) *The Product Manager's Desk Reference*, 1st edition, New York: McGraw-Hill
- https://www.accenture.com/sk-en/insight-understanding-improve-businesses-profitability-analytics.aspx
- http://www.ehow.com/how_7198108_calculate-product-profitability.html

Cash flow analytics

What is it?

Knowing how money is moving in and out of your business (cash flow) and knowing how easy it will be to convert your assets to cash should you need money quickly (liquidity) are essential measures to help you gauge the health, stability and longevity of your business.

Cash flow analytics therefore examines the cash flow in the business and seeks to predict it so that you can avoid problems.

Why does it matter?

Cash flow analytics matter because the day-to-day running of a business requires a certain amount of cash to keep the cogs turning: wages need to be paid, raw materials need to be purchased and suppliers paid. Tracking cash flow so you can appropriately manage it in real time and also prepare for the future is vitally important otherwise you may simply run out of money. And running out of money is one of the most common causes of business failure.

When do I use it?

You should be using cash flow analytics regularly in your business to assess your current position and ensure you have enough money to run your business effectively. In addition, predicting your cash flow needs and expected position in the future can allow you to anticipate and plan for peaks and troughs so they don't end up sideswiping the business.

What business questions is it helping me to answer?

Cash flow analytics can help you to answer many important questions including:

- How much money do I need in the future to run the business effectively?
- Will I have enough cash flow to pay all my bills in time?
- Are there any cash flow trends during the year that I need to manage carefully?

How do I use it?

Retrospective or real-time analysis of cash flow can be achieved by implementing cash flow key performance indicators (KPIs) such as the cash conversion cycle – which calculates the number of days it takes for an organisation to convert resources into cash – working capital ratio, cash flow solvency ratio, cash flow margin and cash flow return on assets.

That said, these KPIs are only looking at what's happened in the past. If you want to predict future cash flow needs then you can use past data to extrapolate into the future if you can identify a trend. Alternatively, you can use tools like regression analysis (Chapter 7) to predict future cash flow.

Practical example

On top of helping a business manage cash flow in real time and also make sure they have enough money to lubricate the business in the future, cash flow analytics can also support a variety of corporate functions.

For example, analytic software can help accounts receivable personnel to increase cash flow by prioritising which customers are contacted by collection staff and when, and also recommend the method of contact most likely to yield success and get the invoices paid.

Tips and traps

Any cash flow analysis is based on data from the past, so it is always important when you are trying to extrapolate data into the future to make the right assumptions. Here is where scenario analysis (Chapter 4) and Monte Carlo simulation (Chapter 13) can help.

Further reading and references

For more information about cash flow analytics see for example:

- Jury, T. (2012) *Cash Flow Analysis and Forecasting: The Definitive Guide to Understanding and Using Published Cash Flow Data*, 1st edition, Hoboken, NJ: Wiley

- Tracy, J.A. and Tracy, T. (2011) *Cash Flow For Dummies*, Hoboken, NJ: Wiley
- http://www.treasuryandrisk.com/2014/02/04/harnessing-predictive-analytics-for-increased-cash
- http://www.ehow.com/info_12009585_can-statement-cash-flows-predict-future-cash-flow.html
- http://www.mindtools.com/pages/article/newTMC_06.htm

32 Value driver analytics

What is it?

Most businesses have a sense of where they are heading and what they are trying to achieve. For many these destinations are formalised on a strategy map that identifies the value drivers in the business. In other words the business has identified the key levers that they need to pull in order to meet their strategic objectives.

Value driver analytics is the assessment and investigation into these levers to ensure that they are actually delivering the expected outcome.

Why does it matter?

Value driver analytics matters because if you are focusing on certain levers and are implementing a certain strategy based on certain assumptions around what those various levers will do, then you absolutely need to test your hypotheses from time to time to make sure your actions are delivering the outcome you want.

If you don't apply analytics to your value drivers then you could simply make assumptions about what aspects of your business will influence and affect other aspects and you may be wrong. If you are wrong, then you are wasting valuable resources focused on the wrong things.

When do I use it?

Apply value driver analytics at least every year, ideally every six months. This will be long enough for you to have some data or evidence as to whether your interventions on the levels you have used in your business are yielding the results you anticipate. For example, you may use price as one of your value drivers and assume that price influences sales and revenue, but you need to test that hypothesis with results so you can establish if you are right or not.

If your hypothesis is correct then you are safe to continue with your chosen strategy, if not then you need to watch the results closely and make alterations to the strategy when necessary.

What business questions is it helping me to answer?

Value driver analytics can help you answer many questions including:

- Are the things we focus on in our business such as lower costs or customer service really delivering the value that we think they are?
- How good are we at delivering value in these key areas?
- Are our product and market strategies delivering the intended results?

How do I use it?

The starting point for implementing value driver analysis is to be really clear about what your value drivers are. You may, for example, believe that you deliver value by reducing costs and serving your customers. That is, in effect, one of your business hypotheses. You then need to build a simple model or construct a business experiment (Chapter 1) that then tests that hypothesis. Scenario analysis (Chapter 4) can also be used to create various possible scenarios around your values to establish whether they really are delivering the results you imagine they do. Correlation analysis (Chapter 3) can also be used here to test the correlation between factors that you believe are connected so that you ensure that X value driver really does influence Y result.

Obviously what happens inside your business is affected by more than just what you do, so you also need to consider external factors such as economic trends or oil price. If you run a transport business the oil price, for example, will have a profound impact on profitability.

Practical example

I worked with a bank who decided that one of their value drivers was customer satisfaction. This was considered very important to the bank and was included as a central theme on their strategy map. And their strategy was to increase customer satisfaction.

By running value driver analytics they were able to identify that they had succeeded and customer satisfaction across the board increased significantly. What they also discovered, however, was that the increased customer satisfaction that they assumed would translate into increased revenue and profit didn't.

They had successfully increased customer satisfaction which was a worthy goal but their efforts did not impact the bottom line at all. Without running this analytics they could have assumed that their efforts were paying financial dividends when they were not.

Tips and traps

The key tip is to properly identify your value drivers and be really clear about what it is you are trying to achieve strategically, even if you start with the key 'stand out' values of your business and test those.

The trap is that you then try to identify all your value drivers and end up trying to create a very complex model. This doesn't actually have to be hard – just stick to the main issues and test your assumptions and assertions about how those things impact your customers and how they impact your business.

Further reading and references

To learn more about value driver analytics see for example:

- Marr, B. (2006) *Strategic Performance Management*, 1st edition, London: Routledge
- Marr, B. (2015) *Big Data*, Hoboken, NJ: Wiley

Shareholder value analytics

33

What is it?

Once a company becomes publicly listed there are certain analytics that will be applied to the business to help investors and analysts decide how strong your business is. The results and interpretation of these tools will influence whether shareholders decide to buy, sell or hold your stock. Shareholder value analytics (SVA) is one of the tools that are commonly used.

SVA is a calculation of the value of a company made by looking at the returns the business provides to its shareholders and effectively measures the financial consequences of strategy. The assumption driving this analysis is that the directors of the business will always seek to maximise shareholder value and wealth.

Why does it matter?

Shareholder value analytics matters because the results and interpretation of the results by investors, analysts and the media will determine how successful your business is on the stock market.

Obviously if the analytics are unfavourable then investors are more likely to sell your shares and buy other shares they consider to be safer or have better results. If the analytics are encouraging then it can increase demand and push the price of your stock up.

When do I use it?

Use shareholder value analytics frequently instead of looking solely at profit and revenue. Profit and revenue can be misleading because profit calculations don't take the cost of equity finance into account so profits can easily be manipulated through creative, albeit legal, accounting practices.

This type of analytics lets the business leaders assess how much value their strategy is actually delivering to the shareholders.

What business questions is it helping me to answer?

Shareholder value analytics can help you answer many questions including:

- Is our strategy working?
- Is the strategy delivering value to the shareholders and if so how much value?
- How does our performance compare with the performance of our competitors?

How do I use it?

In an effort to draw a meaningful distinction between value and profit that would indicate real shareholder value you can use a metric called economic value added (EVA). Basically EVA calculates the profit of a business when the cost of equity finance has been removed because value is only really created when the return on the capital employed is more than the cost of that capital.

Central to EVA are three core ideas: cash is best; 'expenses' such as research and development or staff training are actually investments in disguise; and that equity finance is expensive.

Predicting shareholder value is, however, often more useful because it can help you to manage opinion and the message that goes out to the market so you can maintain stability. There are a range of tools that can help you to apply predictive analytics to shareholder value.

Practical example

The underlying principle of shareholder value analytics is that you will only add value for your shareholders when the returns you make on equity are higher than the costs of that equity. Once the amount of value has been calculated you can then implement targets for improvement and shareholder value can be used as a measure for managing performance. At least that's the theory.

In the early 1970s, Schlitz Brewing's strategy was to reduce brewery labour per barrel. In order to achieve this, Schlitz switched to low-cost hops and halved the brewing cycle. Shareholders were thrilled because shareholder value increased, profits soared and the share price rose to $69.

Unfortunately, shareholder value is not the same as customer value. Although slower to react, by 1976 complaints about the demise in product quality were continual and market share was slipping. Schlitz destroyed 10 million bottles of beer that failed quality control tests in the same year. By the time management tried to get its quality back on track, it was too late and the company couldn't recover.

Having been the second most popular beer in the market their position fell to number seven and their share price dropped to $5.

So while shareholder value may tell you how your strategy is working with your shareholders you also need to analyse customer results too. Ideally you should be seeking to deliver shareholder value and customer value.

Tips and traps

As the practical example demonstrates, shareholder value analytics is not a sure-fire tool to measure success. It needs to be tempered with additional customer-based analysis to ensure that the shareholder value is not occurring at the expense of customer value. Make sure you track customer value alongside shareholder value.

It can also use complex and restrictive assumptions and if thoroughly understood it can be easily manipulated.

Further reading and references

For more about shareholder value analytics see for example:

- Rappaport, A. (1997) *Creating Shareholder Value: A Guide for Managers and Investors*, revised edition, New York: Free Press
- http://www.ias.ac.in/sadhana/Pdf2005AprJun/Pe1306.pdf
- http://www.ehow.com/how_6372049_calculate-shareholder-value.html
- https://hbr.org/1990/03/putting-strategy-into-shareholder-value-analysis
- http://www.cbsnews.com/news/implementing-shareholder-value-analysis/

[PART FOUR]

Market analytics

Unmet need analytics

34

What is it?

Unmet need analytics is the process of uncovering whether there are any unmet needs around your product or service or within your market that you could meet to increase customer satisfaction and revenue.

The purpose is to identify the gap that exists between what the market wants and what your business and/or the market currently provides so your new products or product improvements can close the gap and take advantage of the opportunity.

Why does it matter?

Unmet needs analytics matters because business is all about meeting the needs of customers. Those that do so will usually be successful and those that don't will not survive. There is no point creating a product or service that your market doesn't want or that doesn't fulfil a current need.

It is therefore crucial that you understand the needs of your customers and seek to identify if there is anything your customers want that you are currently not providing them. These insights should direct your product development.

When do I use it?

Customers change, their needs change and the market that you operate within changes. For some businesses those changes will be rapid and frequent. It makes sense therefore to assess your customers' needs and unmet needs at least once a year. Seek to find out if your existing product range is missing the mark with customers or not quite fulfilling their evolving expectations.

Plus, you should apply unmet needs analytics when you are developing new products or services and updating or upgrading your existing product range.

What business questions is it helping me to answer?

Unmet need analytics helps you answer many questions including:

- What new opportunities are there in the market?
- Are your customers gaining all the benefits from your product that they expect?
- Do your customers currently have any unmet needs that your existing products or services are missing?

How do I use it?

Unmet need analysis is the process of finding out what people think and feel about a market, product or service. As such, you could use qualitative surveys (Chapter 20), focus groups (Chapter 21) and interviews (Chapter 22).

Look at what people are searching for online using a tool like Google Trends to help you identify what customers are looking for but may not be currently finding. Google Trends is a public web facility based on Google Searches around the world. It can tell you what is being searched for most frequently in a particular area and in various languages or what topics are trending.

Read feedback from customers online and from customer service calls or product feedback. More and more people leave product reviews and these can shed some light on what your products or services are not currently doing well. Much of this insight will be available in text form or could be converted to text data (Chapter 24) and you could then apply text analytics (Chapter 8) to identify patterns or themes that could identify unmet needs.

Practical example

Sony's Walkman is a classic example of the discovery of an unmet need. When Sony launched the Walkman in 1979 it wasn't a new product. Sony had been promoting a very similar product called the Pressman for some time. Directed at professional journalists the Pressman allowed journalists and reporters to record their interviews and play them back for dictation. It was this playback feature that caught the attention of honorary chairman Masaru Ibuka. He had seen an employee using the Pressman to listen to music and thought it would be a good way to break up the monotony of his frequent air travel. But the device was bulky (and expensive) so he and chairman Akio Morita instructed the head of the tape recording division to make a smaller version.

They modified the Pressman by removing the record function, adding stereo circuits, a headphone terminal and lightweight earphones. The Sony Walkman was born. Since then over 150 million units have been sold around the world filling a previously unmet need – the need to listen to music on the move.

Tips and traps

Most of your customers will be online, they will have social media accounts and probably have a smartphone in their pocket. This means that you have a very direct line of real-time communication with your customers – use it.

It is now very cheap and fast to ask your customers questions. Create forums and online focus groups, or invite customers to like your Facebook page and join a feedback group. Post questions and encourage your customers to share their experiences and tell you if their needs are not being met by your current products.

Too many businesses assume they know why their customers buy their products and what they think of them. Don't assume – ask them directly. And if you do ask, make sure you listen.

Further reading and references

To learn more about unmet need analytics see for example:

- Kim, W.C. and Mauborgne, R. (2015) *Blue Ocean Strategy: How to Create Uncontested Market Space and Make the Competition Irrelevant*, Boston, MA: Harvard Business Review Press
- http://www.businessweek.com/smallbiz/tips/archives/2010/02/to_find_an_unmet_need_use_lead_user_analysis.html
- http://www.google.co.uk/trends/

35 Market size analytics

What is it?

Market size analytics is the process of working out how large the market is for your products and services and whether there is any growth potential. The size of the market is either measured in volume, value or frequency. Volume equates to the number of units sold, value equates to the money spent in that market, and frequency is how often a product is sold. Essentially, the size of a market can be thought of in terms of 'how many', 'how much' and 'how often'.

It seeks to work out how many people want or may want your product or service and how often they may buy it. But the current size of the market is not the only consideration with market size analytics.

Market potential is equally, if not more, important than current size. Just because a market is large does not mean it's profitable – especially if most of the customers that want a particular product or service already have one and are unlikely to want to buy another!

Why does it matter?

Market size analytics matters because if you don't understand the size and potential of your market you can easily jump to conclusions about how viable your business proposition is and waste vast sums of money and time competing in the wrong market or a market that is already reaching saturation point.

Every product or market has a life cycle. Those who enter a particular market first tend to hold an advantage for at least a short time – hence the term 'first-mover advantage'. There is usually a time lag where demand is stronger than supply and those who can supply win. As more and more companies enter the market, competition becomes fierce because consumers have more choice and will become more discerning – seeking a better price. It is essential to know where your products are in their life cycle and whether you are competing in a growing market or a declining market.

When do I use it?

Market size analytics is essential for strategic planning because you need to know in advance whether there are any changes to your market that could impact revenue. If your market is in decline then you need to know about it before it enters the downward phase so that you can price accordingly, and invest in research and development to identify new products and new markets.

Nothing stays the same for long. No business is immune from change. Just because your business is successful today doesn't mean it will automatically be successful tomorrow. You need to know what your market is doing so you can plan ahead and evolve with your customers' needs.

You would also use market size analytics before you invested too heavily in the development of a new product or service. Although you need to keep evolving, you then need to know that what you are evolving to is something that the market wants. There is no point creating a new product for a new market if the market for that product is too small or the market is in decline.

What business questions is it helping me to answer?

Market size analytics helps you answer many questions including:

- What is the demand for our product or service?
- Will there still be demand tomorrow for our product or service?
- Do we need to investigate new markets or new products in order to maintain and grow revenue?
- Is there any upward or downward trend in demand that we need to know about?

How do I use it?

Market size analytics sounds simple but getting your hands on the right data so you can accurately measure market size is not that easy. In order to establish the size of your market you could investigate government data, trade association data or financial data from competitors. In addition you could use customer surveys (Chapter 19 and 20).

It can also be useful to use scenario analysis (Chapter 4) so you can appreciate the outcomes of different moves in the market ahead of time.

The key to really useful market size analytics is to take advantage of all the open data that now exists such as government data. This might include deep demographic data, economic development for specific areas and markets and age profiles. It is also possible to use tools like Google Trends to understand more about what your market is searching for. There is now so much data out there that you don't need to employ a market researcher any more as it's now possible to do a great deal of it yourself by accessing open data that already exists.

Practical example

Say you are a technology manufacturer. You make smart technology but have not yet entered into the Smart TV market. Initially, Smart TVs were a bit of a gimmick. You were not sure if they were going to catch on or quickly be replaced by something else.

So you decide to look more closely at the Smart TV market to decide whether to get involved. Sourcing data from Ofcom, the UK communications regulator, you discover that the size of the Smart TV market is growing rapidly.

This data alerts you to the fact that the Smart TV market is growing at 60 per cent per year! Current market share is 45 per cent, which would indicate this is a strong market to enter. That said, there are already inexpensive USB devices on the market that convert a normal TV into a smart TV so this market may need further investigation.

Tips and traps

Establishing the size of your market can be quite tricky and it can be especially challenging to predict in the future. Even if you can get a sense of how big your market is today and where you sit in that market you will still never know what your competitors will do, or what new products will be launched, or that your customers' needs may change.

Further reading and references

To understand more about market size analytics see for example:

- http://www.netmba.com/marketing/market/analysis/
- http://www.mappinganalytics.com/market-potential/market-potential-sizing.html
- http://www.dummies.com/how-to/content/analysing-your-market-situation.html

Demand forecasting

36

What is it?

Demand forecasting is an area of predictive analytics that seeks to estimate the quantity of a product or service your consumers are likely to buy. As the name suggests, demand forecasting forecasts demand!

Demand forecasting goes beyond educated guesses and looks at historical sales data or current data from test markets. This type of analytic technique is used to direct pricing decisions, assessing future capacity requirements and making strategic decisions regarding new markets.

Why does it matter?

Demand forecasting matters because it provides knowledge on how demand for your products and services fluctuates over time. This data can then be used to manage inventory so that just the right amount of stock is kept on hand to fulfil demand. Clearly if demand isn't forecast or forecasting is done poorly then you are likely to underestimate demand and miss out on sales, or overestimate demand and have a warehouse full of goods that you can't sell. Both will cost you money.

Understanding demand is essential in order to remain competitive because it allows you to control production costs and only make what you know you will sell.

When do I use it?

Demand forecasting is particularly relevant for manufacturers because this information should drive production and influence the price point. There is no point making more and more products when those products then sit in a warehouse for months.

There are, of course, marketing advantages, especially around Christmas, where products are deliberately held back to push up demand, but on the whole it is always best to produce just enough to meet demand and no more, otherwise you waste time, money and resources.

What business questions is it helping me to answer?

Demand forecasting helps you answer business questions such as:

- How many of each product are you likely to sell in the coming months?
- How many of each service you provide are you likely to sell in the coming months?
- How is the demand changing for my products or services?
- What are the trends in demand and are there any consistent peaks and troughs I need to be aware of?

How do I use it?

As the name would suggest, you can forecast demand using forecasting techniques such as time series analysis (Chapter 5). Forecasting is, however, not an exact science, no model is flawless and there is no magical crystal ball. That said, unnecessary costs stemming from too much or too little supply can often be avoided using data mining techniques (Chapter 6). Neural network analysis (Chapter 17) can also be used to forecast demand.

Traditionally, most forecasting was done by looking at past sales but access to new tools and data sets are making this type of analytics much more interesting and accurate. Text analysis on social media posts, product forums and review sites can help to predict demand too. Tools like Google Trends can also help to see what is being discussed, shared and searched for, which can also help predict demand.

By using these types of techniques to forecast demand then you are much more likely to be prepared to meet the actual demands of your customers.

Practical example

Say you are a toy buyer for a major retailer, you will need to forecast demand really well because you need to place your orders with suppliers months in advance. The toys that are on sale at Christmas, for example, will probably have been bought in January, maybe earlier.

Initially, you may start the process by enlisting the help of an expert panel (see focus groups, Chapter 21) to attempt to establish what the big trends will be and what toys the retailer should stock. These insights can then be combined with past sales data and external additional data from social media, toy forums and perhaps toy review sites.

Another great source of information will be the search traffic trends as well as the sales statistics you have access to. These can be used as input for scenario analysis (Chapter 4) or Monte Carlo simulations (Chapter 13).

You might perform a meta-analysis (Chapter 18) to bring together the results of various studies and forecasts. Combining these different data sets will help you to verify results so you can be more confident in the forecasting.

Tips and traps

As with all analytic techniques the adage 'garbage in, garbage out' springs to mind, so the data that you use for data forecasting must be clean and accurate. If it is not then the results will always be skewed and could lead you down the wrong path or strengthen opinion that later turns out to be false.

There are many sources of problem data including data entry issues, although statistical summaries and graphing can often highlight these anomalies. Artificial demand can also provide erroneous data for forecasting purposes. For example, a promotion may temporarily boost sales, but unless you plan to run another promotion then you can't expect or forecast those sales in the future. Plus, uncontrollable external factors such as weather, or seasonal fluctuations can impact demand – all need to be accounted for accurately if the forecast is to be useful.

Further reading and references

To understand more about how to use demand forecasting for your business see for example:

- Chase, C.W. (2009) *Demand-Driven Forecasting: A Structured Approach to Forecasting*, 1st edition, Hoboken, NJ: Wiley
- Thomopoulos, N.T. (2014) *Demand Forecasting for Inventory Control*, New York: Springer
- http://www.statsoft.com/Textbook/Demand-Forecasting
- http://www.ehow.com/info_8425310_forecasting-demand-important.html
- https://www.youtube.com/watch?v=5XYe-8BigRc

37 Market trend analytics

What is it?

Market trend analytics is a process of establishing whether a market is growing, stagnant or in decline and how fast that movement is occurring. Understanding market size is important, but knowing whether that market is trending up or down is also vital for astute strategic and marketing decision making.

Why does it matter?

Market trend analytics matters because you need to know the health and direction your market is heading in.

If you know, for example, that your market is stagnant or in decline then you need to evolve and take action to accommodate that market. You could, for example, create some innovative promotions to kick start the stagnant market or invest in research and development to create new products that can compete in different upward trending markets while you squeeze out the last of the value from the markets you currently operate in.

If you know that your market is growing then you can move resources away from products in declining markets so you can ramp up supply and cash in while the going is good.

When do I use it?

Market trend analytics is something that should be done at least every year, ideally every six months so that you can gauge the direction of the market and make better strategic and tactical decisions as a result.

It's also part of a wider market analysis process when looking to expand or venture into new markets with new or revised products and services.

What business questions is it helping me to answer?

Market trend analytics can help you answer business questions such as:

- Is the market for our goods and services growing, stagnating or in decline?
- Which markets should we focus on for the future?
- Which new markets should we enter, and when?
- Which markets should we abandon, and when?

How do I use it?

To monitor market trends you can run business experiments (Chapter 1) or scenario analysis (Chapter 4) to see what the market would look like and how it would impact your business in either a growing, stagnating or growth market. These types of techniques also help you to see how various degrees of shift in a trend would impact your business.

In addition you can conduct customer surveys (Chapter 19 and 20) or focus groups (Chapter 21) to get a sense of what your customers want and whether there is still an appetite for what you provide.

Practical example

The growing demand for e-cigarettes is a good example of an upwardly trending market. Even though we have known since the 1950s that smoking is very harmful to human health, the big tobacco companies have managed to navigate, question or obfuscate that science so they can continue to profit.

Of course smoking is addictive so even though most people now realise that smoking is killing them, it's difficult to stop. And that's where the e-cigarettes come in. In the space of a few years there is now an e-cigarette shop on every high street.

But no one really knows where that market is going. A smart e-cigarette company could run scenario analysis (Chapter 4) to assess various options based on likely possibilities in the market. It is, for example, highly likely that legislative changes will influence the market sooner rather than later. Smoking e-cigarettes is already banned in restaurants, and chances are more and more places will impose bans as time goes on. This will influence the market and the profitability of the market. They would also be wise to measure customer sentiment on social media and check for an insight on Google Trends to stay on top of the market trends so they are not blindsided by changes they did not see coming.

Tips and traps

Change in any market is inevitable. The trick is knowing what those changes might be before they arrive so you can stay ahead of them, or adapt to meet them and stay competitive.

Every change heralds both an opportunity and a threat. Many also have the potential to dramatically affect the market size and therefore financial viability. Stay mindful of the external environment as well as the internal environment you can control. For example, changes to legislation and social expectations could radically curtail the e-cigarette upward trend.

Although assumed to be healthier than cigarettes, because they are a new product their long-term effect is unknown. There are those that are seeking to limit their use in public and those changes could affect the longevity of the product.

Changes to technology, price sensitivity and changing political conditions can also affect market trends.

Further reading and references

To learn more about market trend analytics see for example:

- Logan, T. (2014) *Profiting from Market Trends: Simple Tools and Techniques for Mastering Trend Analysis*, 1st edition, Hoboken, NJ: Wiley
- http://www.marketingdonut.co.uk/marketing/market-research/market-analysis

Non-customer analytics

38

Non-customer analytics is about understanding what people who are currently not your customers think about your product, services or brand.

Traditionally, we've been told that we need to understand our customers so that we know what they look like and can find more people like them. And while that makes sense there is another group that could be even more important – the non-customer!

Identified by the authors of the *Blue Ocean Strategy*, W. Chan Kim and Renee Mauborgne, the idea is simple but profound. If we identify our ideal customers, and our competitors are doing the same and getting the same profile, then we are all competing for an ever-decreasing slice of an ever-decreasing pie. Price wars begin and the market becomes fiercely competitive as we fight tooth and claw for customer in what becomes a 'red ocean'. Alternatively, we could conduct non-customer analytics to work out who is not buying from us and why so we can move into new, less crowded 'blue ocean' markets.

A 'blue ocean' is an untapped market that has opportunity for growth, higher margins and increased profitability compared with a 'red ocean', which is a highly competitive, crowded market based on price cuts and promotions that savage the bottom line.

According to Kim and Mauborgne there are six assumptions that keep companies trapped in creating red oceans:

1 define their industry similarly and focus on being the best within it;
2 look at their industries through the lens of generally accepted strategic groups and strive to stand out in the strategic group they play in;
3 focus on the same buyer group;
4 define the scope of the products and services offered by their industry similarly;
5 accept their industry's functional or emotional orientation;
6 focus on the same point in time – and often on current competitive threats – in formulating strategy.

Why does it matter?

Non-customer analytics matters because it offers you an opportunity to break this value-cost-trade-off to achieve greater value and lower costs simultaneously. Instead of chasing a dwindling population of increasingly targeted and possibly jaded customers who will insist on discounting, you can identify who is not buying from you and why and expand your market to include those individuals in a less crowded and competitive environment.

If you can find new markets or new pockets within larger markets that have yet to be approached by you or your competitors then you have an opportunity to increase revenue cost-effectively.

When do I use it?

Non-customer analytics is a very useful tool when your market growth or market trend analytics have indicated that you are in a stagnant or declining market. In those circumstances non-customer analytics can help you to identify the three various tiers of 'non-customers' to identify.

First, there are existing customers who are looking to leave or have recently left your business. These would include customers who have not bought from you recently. The second tier is customers who have consciously decided against your product or service. And the third tier consists of customers who are 'distant' to your product or service.

What business questions is it helping me to answer?

Non-customer analytics can help you answer business questions such as:

- Why are customers not buying from you?
- Is there anything in your product or service that is actively putting people off buying your product – if so what?
- Where are the new opportunities for us in the market?

How do I use it?

If you want to know why people are not buying your product or service then you need to ask them. You can run some customer analytics to identify customers who have not bought from you for a certain period of time – say a year – and invite them to complete a questionnaire (Chapter 19 and 20), attend a focus group (Chapter 21) or agree to be interviewed (Chapter 22).

These data collection techniques can also be applied on people who have never been your customer. If you are a top-end car manufacturer such as Mercedes Benz then it would be very useful to speak to Audi or BMW customers to learn why they choose those cars over your own. And this doesn't have to be as difficult as it may initially sound. We live in a world where people are sharing their life online. The purchase of a new car will almost certainly be included on a Facebook timeline or Twitter post and those people can now quite easily be identified and approached. The car manufacturer could create a#tag on Twitter such as #WhyNotMercedes and invite competitor's customers to provide feedback.

Practical example

The potential of non-customer analysis was illustrated by the authors of *Blue Ocean Strategy* using Cirque du Soleil as an example.

Prior to Cirque du Soleil the circus industry consisted of two types – large, big-name productions such as the Ringing Brothers that offered a high-end product, and small regional touring companies that offered a less impressive experience but at a much lower cost. The major costs for a circus are the circus animals and the talent.

They didn't want to compete in an already crowded market at either end of the spectrum. They determined that they could eliminate the major costs by not involving animals, which was controversial anyway, and big-name talent. They looked at other industries and adapted their show accordingly. The end result was a spectacular acrobatics show with story themes and lots of showbusiness razzle dazzle. In doing so they created a new market – a new blue ocean market, reaching a whole new audience who would never have considered attending a traditional circus show.

Tips and traps

It can be remarkably easy to get feedback from people who are not your customers using the power of social media.

The biggest trap that analysts fall into with non-customer analytics is that they ask customers. Although this can be useful when asking lapsed customers, the idea is to go beyond your traditional market and find people who would not normally buy what you are selling, so you need to find those people and ask them for their opinion so that you can gain useful insights.

Further reading and references

To understand more about non-customer analytics see for example:

- Kim, W.C. and Mauborgne, R. (2015) *Blue Ocean Strategy: How to Create Uncontested Market Space and Make the Competition Irrelevant*, Boston, MA: Harvard Business Review Press
- http://matthopkins.com/business/the-non-customer/

39 Competitor analytics

What is it?

Competitor analytics is important for marketing and strategic planning. It allows you to understand your competitors in more than just a cursory ad hoc way. Not everyone in your market is your competitor; some may sell similar products but to a different audience and some may simply be too small to be your competitors. You need to know who your real competitors are, how they are positioned in the market and in relation to your business.

By understanding their strengths and weaknesses you can identify opportunities to exploit and threats to navigate or mitigate through strategic planning. Plus, competitor analytics pulls all the relevant information on all your competitors together so that you can see the whole picture not just snapshots when you focus on one main competitor.

Why does it matter?

Competitor analytics matters because your business does not exist in a vacuum. It is part of a dynamic industry where many businesses are all seeking the same consumer spend. If you are to prosper in that dynamic market you need to know what's happening around you and how you and your competitors are perceived by the market.

Competitor analytics help you to understand your competitive advantages and disadvantages relative to your competition. It also helps you to predict what they will do in the future and therefore how you can stay ahead. Plus, if you know how they have behaved in the past you can better predict how they will behave in the future and how they may respond to a new product or pricing strategy.

When do I use it?

This depends on how changeable your industry is. If there are constantly new companies entering your market and others falling away then you would be wise to conduct thorough competitor analytics at least once a year. If the industry is fairly stable and your main competitors haven't changed in several years then once every couple of years will probably be enough.

That said, you do need to review your findings when you are making important strategic decisions. That way you can anticipate what your competitors will do if your plans will impact them and how you can counter any competitive move.

What business questions is it helping me to answer?

Competitor analytics will help you answer some important business questions including:

- Who are our key competitors and why?
- What are the objectives of our key competitors and how does that differ from our objective?
- What are their strengths and weaknesses?
- What threats do they pose?
- What opportunities do they present?
- What strategies are they pursuing and how would they affect us?
- Based on their past action how are they likely to respond to changes in our business?

How do I use it?

As always, strong and useful analytics relies on strong and useful information. You can source competitor data from recorded data that is easily available such as annual reports, product brochures and marketing activity. If possible, have an employee, friend or family member to buy a product or service from your key competitors and assess their experience. This will also get that person on their mailing list so you can see all their communication and marketing efforts. Pay attention to business journals and newspapers for any mention of your competitors. You can use media monitor services to find these or simply create a Google Alert which will alert you to any online mention of your competitor.

There is also observable data which is collected from various sources such as competitor pricing data, advertising campaigns, etc. And finally, there is opportunistic data such as trade shows, supplier meetings, and sales force meetings. Your sales team will often meet would-be clients who are already doing business with your competitors – they could be a rich source of information.

This type of analytics used to be quite laborious but so much data already exists online. You can, for example, read competitor product reviews like their Facebook page and see what their customers are saying about them. When you have the data you could conduct text analytics (Chapter 8) and sentiment analysis (Chapter 9) to gain insights into what your competitors are doing right and doing wrong.

Practical example

Say you are a mobile phone manufacturer and you wanted to conduct competitor analytics. The easiest way to start would be to use the internet to establish all the other companies that manufacture mobile phones. Most businesses already know who their main competitors are but may not know all their competitors, or may not consider companies that create products that are a substitute for their product. Today more and more people are using tablets or simply making calls via services such as Skype – these are also therefore competitors because they could and do replace the need for a phone at all. So Skype may be an indirect competitor of yours and certainly what that business is doing should be something you know about.

Once you've compiled your list of key competitors and indirect competitors you need to identify the key value drivers in the market. What do customers in this market value the most? What are the features and benefits they are searching for when they buy their product? Are they interested primarily in price, quality, length of warranty, simplicity to operate, etc.? Looking at your own customer analytics can help establish what those features may be. Once you have a full list of features and benefits identify which competitor fulfils which ones. Of course it may be easy to figure out if a competitor product has a particular feature or not, but benefits are more subjective. However, if you look at social media data, for example from review sites, you will be able to establish if each competitor delivers certain benefits too.

Finally, you need to compare your own offering to your competitors – especially your top three rivals and work out what makes you products or services unique. Are those factors important? Do your customers know about them, do they recognise the difference? Again there is a wealth of new data such as social media data and review data that can tell you a great deal about your competition and what their customers think about their products. And all of this data can be broken down by service, product, competitor or geographic location.

Tips and traps

The most useful tip for competitor analytics is to do it! Most businesses don't. Instead they think they have analysed their competitors because they may share snippets of information that a manager might hear at a conference or they may notice a newspaper article and share that in a strategic meeting. And yet this approach places your business at risk of potentially dangerous competitor blind spots.

Don't fall into the trap of thinking that informal impressions, intuition and conjecture is a) all you need and b) competitor analytics. The process is much more systematic and thorough than that, and if you invest the time it will yield reward and inform your decision making.

Further reading and references

To find out more about competitor analytics see for example:

- Carrel, J. and Everitt, R. (2012) *Easy Competitor Analysis – How To Find What Your Competitors Are Up To & How To Benefit From That Valuable Knowledge*, 1st edition, Bury St Edmunds: Cinnamon Edge Publishing
- Hall, D. (2014) *Online Competitive Analysis: Identify the strengths & weaknesses of your online competitors and learn how to outperform them!*, The SEO Effect
- http://edwardlowe.org/digital-library/how-to-conduct-and-prepare-a-competitive-analysis/
- http://hostopiablog.verticalresponse.com/blog/quick-and-savvy-competitive-analysis/
- http://www.netmba.com/strategy/competitor-analysis/
- http://competitoranalysis.com/
- http://sherpablog.marketingsherpa.com/research-and-measurement/competitive-analysis-tools/
- http://www.coursework4you.co.uk/essays-and-dissertations/competitor-analysis.php

40 Pricing analytics

What is it?

Pricing analytics is the process of analysing price sensitivity in market segments and it is one of the critical territories of business analytics. Pricing analytics has emerged as an important tool to increase profitability, especially in highly competitive markets where everything that can be done has been done.

How much you charge for your products and services will depend on your pricing strategy and whether you are selling low cost high volume, or high cost low volume – or some compromise in between. Traditionally, companies have priced their products and services using a couple of methods: they either calculate their fixed and variable costs to establish how much it costs the business to supply those products or services and add a margin on top as profit; or they don't compete on price and set a significantly higher price than production hoping that they will sell enough to cover costs. In both cases the business will probably pay close attention to what the competition is charging and stay within an acceptable range.

But what if you could find out exactly how much your customers would pay for your product ahead of time? Price analytics is the process that delivers that outcome.

Why does it matter?

Price analytics matters because it allows you to drive incremental sales and profit in tight markets. In the past no one really knew how much a customer would have been willing to pay for the product or service they bought. And yet if the price was set too low then you've missed out on profit; too high and you miss out on the sale altogether. There is therefore a fine line and that line shifts all the time depending on each individual customer.

Pricing analytics allows you to tailor your pricing to different segments of your market so you can capitalise on the 'low hanging fruit' and those who are willing to pay more for your product or service. As a result you can increase volume and profit margin which therefore positively impacts revenue simply by using some clever pricing analytics.

With more and more pricing information available in real time, companies can also dynamically adjust prices and match competitors in real time when they increase or decrease their prices.

When do I use it?

The potential benefits of pricing analytics are such that you should use this tool consistently. When assessed on a regular basis the insights it provides allow you to manage your pricing for maximum revenue.

And considering that the insights don't require any further action or initiative other than a change to the price of your product, it's a cost-effective and relatively simple way to increase profit.

What business questions is it helping me to answer?

Pricing analytics can help you answer business questions such as:

- What's the optimum price to charge to maximise sales and profits?
- Does that price vary according to market segments?
- How can I create price tiers to maximise revenue?
- How do I optimise my dynamic pricing?

How do I use it?

Pricing analytics looks at what's happened in the past, but more importantly what is likely to happen in the future. This requires data mining (Chapter 6) and the development of forecasting models and algorithms (Chapter 5).

In addition, it often involves multiple, concurrent business experiments (Chapter 1) that can be run quickly and easily time and time again, so you can measure what is likely to happen with each price change.

Practical example

The insurance industry is a big user of pricing analytics. Insurance is a notoriously volatile and changeable product. For most insurance companies margins are dwindling and competition is fierce.

The holy grail is to sell insurance and encourage the customer to elect for automatic renewal. If you have ever elected for automatic renewal – you should know that the insurance company you've bought your policy from has almost certainly applied pricing analytics to figure out how much they can raise your premium each year without triggering a cancelation.

What makes pricing analytics so exciting now is that so much of the necessary data is in the public domain. This data is, for example, already widely used in supermarkets. Most supermarkets offer some sort of price match service to stop their customers 'shopping around'. If a customer buys a product that they could have bought cheaper at a rival supermarket then the customer is given a money-off coupon for the value of the difference that they can then use the next time they visit. This is all made possible by price data in the public domain.

There are now third party data specialists that can give you access to this data for a fraction of the cost were you to compile it yourself – and it's kept very accurate and up to date. You can then use this data to analyse your pricing against your competitors.

Tips and traps

Chances are that now you know that your insurance company is deliberately squeezing more money from you each year for the same product you might be a little ticked off. Most people are when they understand this analytic process. And insurance is by no means the only sector using this technique. The danger of course is that customers find out about it and feel cheated. Insurance companies for example are in effect taking advantage of their loyal customers. They are making their loyal customers pay more and giving the better deals to those that shop around. This also happens frequently in the banking sector but customers are becoming increasingly aware of the practice.

If you use pricing analytics to improve revenue, make sure you improve the value you add to customers that are paying a little more. Ideally offer them something additional that doesn't cost you any money to deliver. That way those customers who are paying more are also getting a little more, or at least the perception of greater value.

Further reading and references

To understand more about pricing analytics see for example:

- Sorger, S. (2013) *Marketing Analytics: Strategic Models and Metrics*, 1st edition CreateSpace Independent Publishing Platform
- http://mma.com/expertise/pricing-analytics/
- http://www.accenture.com/us-en/outlook/Pages/outlook-journal-2011-allure-of-predictive-pricing.aspx

Marketing channel analytics

41

What is it?

Marketing channel analytics allows you to assess the different marketing channels available to you and establish which are the most effective. The ideal marketing channel will always be influenced by costs, the demographic of the customer you are seeking to reach and also what your competitors are doing, among other things.

It is likely that you will reach different segments of your market via different channels, but it is still crucial that you know which ones are working and which ones are less effective so you can make better marketing decisions.

Why does it matter?

Marketing channel analytics matters because there are literally hundreds of possible channels and ways to market your products and services. These range from the traditional print ads, PR, media and direct marketing to home shopping networks, guerrilla marketing tactics, giveaways to online marketing as well as social media and mobile. There is only so much time in the day and only so much money available for marketing so understanding which is going to deliver most bang for your buck is essential.

Marketing channel analytics looks at costs and return on investment so that the marketing budget can be used more effectively.

When do I use it?

It is a good idea to start with a complete analysis of all marketing activity and then create a process for a more ongoing review.

What business questions is it helping me to answer?

Marketing channel analytics can help you answer business questions such as:

- What type of marketing is more cost-effective for reaching our customers?
- Is online marketing more effective than offline marketing?
- Are our prospects or customers doing what we want them to do as a result of the advertising?
- What marketing channel is most effective?
- What marketing channel is most profitable?

How do I use it?

The first step is to list all your current and potential marketing channels. You need to be clear about what it is you are trying to achieve with each channel. So for print advertising you might want customers to call you using the number on the advert. With online marketing you may want the customer to click through to your website or click on a banner advert. Or that may not be enough for you – you may want the customer to then add a product to their shopping basket and complete the purchase.

For each of the current marketing channels, and any potential as yet unused channels, set some conversion rate goals so you know what you want that channel to deliver.

Too often businesses launch themselves into a particular marketing channel without any real idea of what success will look like for them in that channel. And this is why there is the old marketing adage – '50 per cent of all marketing spend is wasted but the problem is we don't know which 50 per cent'. We don't know which 50 per cent because we don't conduct marketing channel analytics and have clear targets for the channel before we begin.

And there really is no excuse for not conducting this analysis any more as so much data is available – especially online to help assess results. Advertising with companies like Facebook, LinkedIn and Twitter have integrated analytics included in the advertising so that you know what happens as a result of that advertising. And in many cases you only pay for the clicks that result in the meeting of your specified goal, i.e. make a purchase, complete a survey or sign up to a newsletter. And all this data is then available to analyse using web analytics (Chapter 47) or data mining (Chapter 6) to extract further insights.

Practical example

Marketing channel analytics is not just about identifying the best-performing platforms but also the most cost-effective.

Say your marketing channel analytics discovered that the most effective method of marketing that you currently use is direct marketing. Your campaigns consistently yield high response rates and generate significant return on investment; a reasonably close second is your online promotions.

When you take costs into consideration, however, the online promotions are a clear winner because although they don't yield as much income they are much cheaper to implement. Direct marketing is expensive whereas online promotions are not.

Tips and traps

Market channel analytics is obviously easier online than offline. Online marketing channels are digital and often the analytics are built into the marketing platform. Effectiveness of offline channels such as direct marketing have used different codes on response forms but offline channels are also benefiting from new technology and tools. For example, retailers can put sensors in shop mannequins to count passing traffic, how many people look at the window display and who then enters the shop.

The biggest trap with marketing channel analytics is that by definition you are assessing the channels in isolation. And that might be quite misleading. For example, if I measure the success of my email marketing campaign and it looks positive, I have no way of knowing how many of those customers have already been on my website or seen a few of my blogs or read some of my books *prior* to getting that email. The email campaign will be credited with the positive outcome, but it might not have been the email campaign alone that caused the outcome. There are now tools that can help to appreciate these interconnections and influences such as multi-channel funnels which show how marketing channels work together to create sales and conversions.

Further reading and references

To find out more about marketing channel analytics see for example:

- Palmatier, R. and Stern, L. (2014) *Marketing Channel Strategy*, 8th edition, Englewood Cliffs, NJ: Prentice Hall
- http://www.studylecturenotes.com/mba-marketing/marketing-distribution-channel-analysis
- http://www.ehow.com/info_8707503_distribution-channels-marketing-analysis.html
- http://www.ukessays.com/essays/marketing/the-distribution-channel-and-market-analysis-marketing-essay.php
- https://support.google.com/analytics/answer/1191180?hl=en
- http://www.hubspot.com/products/analytics

42 Brand analytics

Brand analytics seeks to determine the strength of your brand compared to your competitors. Your brand is more than just your logo and your commercial livery; it's the look and feel of your products and what they represent to your customers.

Contrary to popular opinion your brand is not what you think it is; it's what your customer thinks it is and, more importantly, what Google and other search engines think it is. Knowing what that is, is clearly important and will impact your decision making and strategic direction.

The purpose of brand analytics is to:

- Find out your current market position and what your brand stands for according to your customers and other external sources.
- Investigate your current and future internal brand according to your management and employees.
- If a gap exists between the two – take action to close that gap.

Why does it matter?

Brand analytics matters because brands matter, and what your customers think and feel about your business and brand matters because it will often influence whether they buy your product or not.

Brand fashions may come and go and if your product or service is the current 'must have' product then ride the wave, but even if it's not you need to understand what you are selling above and beyond the product or service. Is your brand young, innovative and creative? Is it secure and strong? Does it spell trust? Knowing these things can make a huge difference to performance and how you position and market your offerings.

When do I use it?

Brand analytics is something that needs to be monitored. Thankfully this is much easier than it used to be because of social media. Many companies are not monitoring what is being said about them and therefore what their customers think of their brand via social media posts on Facebook and Twitter.

For example, the sports drink company Gatorade has had a social media command centre in Chicago since 2010. 'Mission Control' is a marketing 'war room' housed inside the marketing department and it monitors the brand in real time. Gatorade measures blog conversations across a variety of topics and shows how hot those conversations are across the blogosphere. The company also runs detailed analysis around key topics and product and campaign launches. It also tracks terms relating to its brand, including competitors, as well as its athletes and sports nutrition-related topics. Basically, Gatorade knows what people are saying about the company and its products all over the world.

What business questions is it helping me to answer?

Brand analytics can help you answer business questions such as:

- What do our customers think of our brand?
- Is that impression changing over time?
- What are they saying about competitors compared to us?

How do I use it?

Brand analytics is about understanding how your brand is perceived. In order to do that you can source data anywhere your customers and potential customers are discussing your brand. This could include customer service conversations, sales conversations, online forums, blogs, review sites, and social media. You can also install Google Alerts, which will alert you every time someone mentions your brand online.

Once you have the base information via text or voice data you can then apply sentiment analysis (Chapter 9) to keep an eye on whether the overall mood is positive or negative towards your brand.

Practical example

As the owner of a local chain of gyms and fitness centres you are keen to understand how your brand is perceived. This is not the first time you analysed your brand. A few years after starting the business you employed a brand consultant who did the research for you. This included focus groups (Chapter 21) as well as various surveys (Chapter 19 and 20) and in-depth interviews (Chapter 22). This was, however, quite time-consuming and expensive.

This time you want to use some of the new data sets that already exist and conduct the analysis yourself. You start by putting your brand into various search engines and seeing what comes up about your brand. Following links and visiting review sites can allow you to see what others are saying about your business and brand. All the text data you discover will then allow you to run sentiment analysis (Chapter 9) so you can gauge how people feel about your brand, and also text analysis (Chapter 8) to see what they are saying about your brand. There is now so much data online and people are so comfortable (for better or worse) sharing their experiences online that you can easily access data that will help assess your brand. Plus, this data is already out there – it's recent and usually more honest and accurate than many of the traditional approaches.

Tips and traps

The internet is a rich source of information regarding how people feel about your brand and your business. People love to share, they especially love to share when someone has upset them, or they are upset about a product or service. You need to tap into this rich vein of information so you can monitor the health of your brand and use the feedback as an opportunity to improve and quickly convert unhappy customers into raving fans.

Ironically, if you solve a customer's problem quickly you have an opportunity to not only turn that situation around but win them over completely.

You can, however, get lost down a rabbit warren of data if you are not careful. This process is not simply seeking to find out what everyone has ever said about your brand, it's about gauging the sentiment and how people perceive your brand so you can take action where necessary to improve that perception and add brand value.

Further reading and references

To find out more about brand analytics see for example:

- Sorger, S. (2013) *Marketing Analytics: Strategic Models and Metrics*, 1st edition, CreateSpace Independent Publishing Platform
- http://www.tcba.co.uk/

[PART FIVE]

Customer analytics

Customer satisfaction analysis

43

What is it?

Customer satisfaction analysis is the process of assessing whether your customers are getting what they want and expect from your business, product or service. In essence, are they satisfied or unsatisfied with their experience of buying from you, or your product or service?

Measuring customer satisfaction is one of the most common forms of business analysis that companies engage in beyond financial analysis. It allows you to find out exactly what parts of your product or service are most appreciated by your customers. Too many businesses have got into financial trouble because they have made inaccurate assumptions about what their customers want, need or love.

Done properly, customer satisfaction analysis can be an extremely insightful management tool because it helps to illustrate any gaps that may exist between current delivery and customer expectations. As such, it allows a business to close that gap more quickly and improve customer satisfaction in the process.

Why does it matter?

Customer satisfaction matters because, generally speaking, customers who are happy with your product or service and have enjoyed a smooth and problem-free buying experience are much more likely to buy from you again and become a loyal and profitable customer.

Maintaining plenty of satisfied customers also helps to keep costs down because it's significantly more expensive to attract new customers than it is to keep the ones you already have. It makes sense therefore to measure customer satisfaction so you know what your customers think and feel about your business, product and brand so you know whether or not you are on track or you are losing too many customers to your competitors.

Plus, in the past if you managed to irritate the odd customer you might receive the occasional angry phone call or terse letter, but it wasn't the end of the world. Not any more! An unsatisfied customer can wreak havoc with your brand and post derogatory reviews that will and do have an impact on future sales. You need to know how happy or otherwise your customers are in real time so you can take action to ensure as many as possible are as happy as possible.

When do I use it?

Measuring customer satisfaction should be an ongoing process because the insights represent a huge potential opportunity or threat depending on how effective the analysis is and how often you engage in the analysis.

Having an unhappy customer is not necessarily a bad thing. It's part of business life and should be expected. How you as a business then handle that customer, however, can determine whether or not that customer turns into a threat or an opportunity.

I have a colleague who bought a modern but retro record player as a Christmas present. It was one that could also play CDs, plug in an MP3 player as well as play and record vinyl. It arrived on time and looked fantastic. The problem was that it would turn itself off every now and again. It was quite easily fixed and would start again immediately but it wasn't ideal. My colleague was obviously disappointed and contacted the seller. The seller told her that there were no replacements, she would be issued with a full refund including postage and could keep or dispose of the product as she saw fit. That's customer service! My colleague went from being very dissatisfied to be a raving fan of this company in a heartbeat. The business may have lost that sale but she will buy from them again, and she has since posted glowing reviews on their website and provides feedback that will appear on Amazon which will almost certainly drive additional future sales to that business.

Dissatisfaction is not in itself bad. The key is being aware of it quickly enough so that you can take the necessary action to turn dissatisfied customers into satisfied customers and ensure that more are the latter instead of the former. That can only be achieved if you engage in customer satisfaction analytics regularly.

What business questions is it helping me to answer?

Customer satisfaction analytics helps you answer business questions such as:

- Are we providing what our customers want?
- Are they happy with the products and services we offer?
- Are our customers satisfied with the service we provide?
- How well are we satisfying our customers?

How do I use it?

Satisfaction is a subjective term which means that not everyone will be satisfied by the same things. This can make the analysis of satisfaction tricky. The most common ways are a combination of quantitative and qualitative surveys (Chapter 19 and 20). The quantitative element, i.e. 'on a scale of 1–5 (1 being very dissatisfied and 5 being very satisfied) how satisfied are you with X', provides data which will allow you to indicate the customer satisfaction trend over time, whereas the qualitative element will dig deeper into those ranked scores to help you better understand the dynamics of satisfaction.

It is also possible to create a customer satisfaction index (CSI). A CSI is simply an average of all the attributes that you believe contribute to customer satisfaction. It is always advisable not to assume what those attributes are and focus groups (Chapter 21) and factor analysis (Chapter 16) can be particularly useful in figuring out all the various aspects of your product and service that a wide variety of your customers appreciate.

Once you know the various factors you then weight them. For example, customer satisfaction for an airline may include on-time departure, quick transit through security, aircraft safety and on-board snacks. Clearly the quality of on-board snacks adds to the sense of satisfaction a customer may experience, but it's probably not considered as crucial as on-time departure or aircraft safety! As a result, the attributes need to be weighted to account for their varying importance.

The customer satisfaction index can therefore be a single score generated from your own unique index of factors you've identified influence satisfaction for your customers, or you can use an existing index.

The widely used American Customer Satisfaction Index (ACSI) or the National Customer Satisfaction Index-UK generates a single score based on drivers of satisfaction such as customer expectations, perceived quality, perceived value, customer complaints, customer retention, customer loyalty and price tolerance.

The beauty of these existing tools is that they ask the same questions (tailored slightly to each industry), which means that you can compare your business to others in your sector and to your nearest competition.

In addition to these traditional tools there are now many new, often relatively inexpensive, ways to analyse customer satisfaction using the plethora of new data sets that now exist. For example, you probably post reviews, post on product forums, create Facebook posts about your product or tweet about your product, service or business. Not only is this data already out there but it's also untainted by research conditions – what your customers say about you online is probably the closest you'll get to the truth. As a result, that text data can be retrieved and analysed to gauge sentiment (Chapter 8 and 9).

Practical example

Many large companies such as Gatorade and Dell track what their customers are saying about them in real time. They monitor social media including Facebook and Twitter, blogs and all types of online discussions. In the same way the CIA can monitor conversation traffic to identify key words of phrases that may alert them to a potential threat we can now monitor whenever anyone mentions a particular product, brand or business. Even something as accessible and simple to use as Google Alerts can tell you whenever someone mentions your name online or mentions a product or brand!

By accessing data that is already in existence you can then use text analytics to analyse customer satisfaction and sentiment analysis to gauge whether the sentiment towards your product or service is generally positive or negative. Plus, there is also some very exciting predictive capabilities with this data.

As already mentioned, researchers at the Microsoft Research Labs in Redmond, Washington, discovered that it was possible to predict which women were at risk of postnatal depression just by analysing their Twitter posts (see Chapter 9, sentiment analysis). Instead of using an algorithm that looked at searches or purchases of the mother, the research focused on the language and words the mother used in social media posts prior to giving birth.

If this can be done to identify those at risk of postnatal depression before it occurs and therefore offer additional support to prevent it occurring, then there is no reason why it can't be used to identify customers at the risk of leaving a business or bailing out to the competition.

Being able to track customer satisfaction in real time is now possible through the vast amount of data that is being created and shared online. These insights can help you stay one step ahead of your customers so that you consistently deliver what they want and need.

Tips and traps

There really is no need to invest in potentially expensive surveys when there is probably already a plethora of qualitative data that exposes your customer satisfaction. Encourage your customers to interact with you via your Facebook page or Twitter – that data can then be used to improve your business and increase revenue.

The main trap to be mindful of with customer satisfaction is that even if a customer is satisfied – even very satisfied – that satisfaction does not always convert into profit. And it certainly doesn't necessarily translate into loyalty.

Further reading and references

To understand more about customer satisfaction analysis see for example:

- Hayes, B.E. (2008) *Measuring Customer Satisfaction and Loyalty: Survey Design, Use, and Statistical Analysis Methods*, 3rd edition, Milwaukee, WI: ASQ Press
- Denove, C. and Power, J. (2007) *Satisfaction: How Every Great Company Listens to the Voice of the Customer*, New York: Portfolio

- Allen, D.R. and Rao, T.R.N. (2000) *Analysis of Customer Satisfaction Data*, Milwaukee, WI: ASQ Press
- http://marketing.gfkamerica.com/website/articles/Customer_Sat_Analysis.pdf
- http://www.decisionanalyst.com/services/satisfaction.dai
- http://www.mineful.com/customer-analysis/customer-satisfaction-index.html
- http://whitespaceanalysis.com/uploads/files/Using_Regression_In_Customer_Experience_Analysis.pdf

44 Customer lifetime value analytics

What is it?

Customer lifetime value analytics is the process of analysing how valuable the customer is to the business over the entire lifetime of the relationship. Instead of looking at transaction profitability this tool seeks to establish how long a customer is likely to stay a customer, how often they are likely to buy during that period and therefore how valuable they are across that time frame.

For some companies a customer may be profitable as soon as they make their first purchase. For others they may only become profitable after several purchases. Clearly it's important to know which camp your customers fall into.

Why does it matter?

Customer lifetime value analytics matters because it allows you to attribute a lifetime value to each customer so you can immediately see which ones are the most valuable and therefore most important to you. This insight can allow you to focus your marketing attention on those customers that are most likely to buy.

It also provides insight for the sales and marketing department because if you know how much a customer is worth to your business over the lifetime of the relationship, this information will then direct how much you can afford to spend in attracting that customer in the first place.

It may be, for example, worth discounting early on or providing a welcome offer to secure the customer because you know that in the long run they will be profitable. Without customer lifetime analytics these types of decisions can often be made on gut feeling or assumption, which can be disastrous for the bottom line.

When do I use it?

How often you should engage in customer lifetime analytics will depend on your industry. For example, banking used to enjoy a very long customer lifetime and therefore there was plenty of time to accumulate profit. Most people would bank with the same bank that their parents set up a bank account with when they were children! Besides, switching bank accounts was awkward and tedious because it often meant changing direct debits and informing lots of different companies or organisations. As a result, even if the service was *really* bad most customers would just stay anyway. That's not the case any more and new legislation and bank requirements mean they now need to make it very easy to switch bank accounts. This has started to change the length of customer relationships to their bank. The same thing is also happening in insurance where we are much happier to shop around and find the best deal.

In industries such as mobile phones the lifetime of a customer relationship can be as little as a couple of years, i.e. often the minimum length of the contract. At a minimum you need to conduct customer lifetime analytics at least once a year to see if there has been any change in the length of the relationship and the buying behaviour and profitability of your customers.

What business questions is it helping me to answer?

Customer lifetime value analytics helps you answer business questions such as:

- How well do we understand the financial value from our customer relationships?
- How long do our customers stay with us?
- What is the average length of our customer relationships?
- What is the average lifetime value of our customer relationships?

How do I use it?

Once you know customer lifetime value you can run regression analysis (Chapter 7) to establish what factors influence the length of customer relationship or the total value of that relationship. The idea is to identify ways to increase the length of the relationship and the value of the customer.

Companies are now also able to bring diverse data sets together around each customer to build a more holistic picture of the customer. In the past, companies with different product lines would store their customer information separately so that one customer may show up three or four times on different systems in the business based on the different products or services they bought. Now with big data analytic techniques, increased storage and processing ability all that disparate data can be collated in one place to profile customers more effectively and make better decisions based on that information.

Practical example

I helped one telecommunications company to develop customer lifetime value analytics so they could figure out how much to spend to get a new customer.

The telecom market is completely saturated so the only way to grow their business was to steal customers from their competitors, but they didn't know how long the average customer stayed with them and they didn't know how much the average customer spent with them and therefore how profitable each customer was.

Without that information they were not sure if their marketing was genuinely effective and they certainly didn't know how much they could afford to spend in order to lure customers away from their competitors and keep them for long enough to make that investment pay off.

Customer lifetime analytics changed all that and their business is still going from strength to strength.

Tips and traps

The biggest challenge with lifetime value is finding the right formula for your business. No single formula is 100 per cent accurate; whatever you end up with it will never be perfect, but don't get hung up on that.

Also, you really need to understand your customers properly, and that can be challenging for many businesses whose internal systems make it impossible to appreciate that one customer may actually use several of your products. And if you don't know that then you can miss the genuine lifetime value of that customer.

Further reading and references

To find out more about customer lifetime value analytics see for example:

- Miller, T.W. (2015) *Marketing Data Science: Modeling Techniques in Predictive Analytics with R and Python*, 1st edition, Upper Saddle River, NJ: Pearson Education
- http://www.insead.edu/facultyresearch/research/doc.cfm?did=51835
- http://www.anderson.ucla.edu/faculty/dominique.hanssens/content/JSR2006.pdf
- http://www.mineful.com/customer-analysis/customer-lifetime-value.html
- http://hbswk.hbs.edu/archive/1436.html

Customer segmentation analytics

45

What is it?

Customer segmentation analytics is the process of finding sub-groups or segments within the overall market. Traditionally, this type of analysis was used in direct marketing where the target audience was sliced up based on geographic, demographic or psychographic information so as to target smaller sub-groups with particular offers that would be most appealing to that segment of the market.

Being able to assess all your customers and split them up into various segments that might buy more of one product than another or buy more often allows you to tailor your marketing and communication efforts. These segments then benefit from a customised marketing plan which helps to increase customer satisfaction as they are only marketing to customers about the things they are interested in. It also reduces costs because you are not marketing to people who have no interest in that product or service, the combination of which means you spend less money to make more money.

Why does it matter?

Seeking to sell all things to all customers via the 'shotgun' approach doesn't work and is very expensive. Customer segmentation analytics is the analysis that can prevent that waste and help you meet your customer needs better while increasing profit.

Customer segmentation analysis allows you to detect the various sub-groups within the market so you can better understand your customers, learn about the clusters within the customer base and customise your approach to maximise sales. It also allows you to find your most profitable customer segments so you can deliberately focus on keeping those customers and attracting more of those types of customer.

Plus, this technique allows you to see who are the least valuable customer segments so that you can actively avoid pursuing those types of customer and not waste too many resources trying to keep them.

When do I use it?

Customer segmentation analytics needs to be ongoing. You should know the segments of you customer base all the time as these insights should be directing your marketing efforts.

Ideally you should conduct customer segmentation analytics before a major marketing initiative to ensure your audience is the right audience for the campaign.

Depending on the volatility of your industry and how often your customer base changes, it may be enough to conduct this analysis once a year.

What business questions is it helping me to answer?

Customer segmentation analytics helps you answer business questions such as:

- Does our customer base break down into sub-groups of customers that share useful characteristics?
- Is it possible to reduce our marketing spend by only targeting those customers who are most likely to buy a particular product or service?
- Do our customers exhibit certain buying behaviour that we can exploit?

How do I use it?

In the past we have been quite limited in the way we can segment the customer base. Traditionally, that would have included where the customer lives, their previous buying history, and their age or gender. It wasn't terribly sophisticated.

Now we are able to segment customers in entirely new ways because we have access to so much information. We don't just have the information we hold about the customer any more – the internet is a vast source of additional data that will help us build a picture of our customers for further segmentation and more accurate targeting. This can be achieved thought text analytics (Chapter 8) and also data mining (Chapter 6).

Once we have the data we can use data mining tools to process millions of records, with millions of data points and variables to detect previously undetectable patterns.

Theoretically you could slice and dice your market in many different ways. But this is not always effective. When you find patterns and identify potential new segments to market, ask yourself six question to test the validity of the segment:

1 Are the segments distinct and identifiable? The groups you identify should be sufficiently different on variables that can be measured now and in the future.

2 Are the segments you identify sizable? There is no point identifying a killer segment with three people in it! Unless you are selling aircraft carriers, marketing to small segments will not be viable.

3 Are the segments reachable? There is no point identifying a segment if the identifier can be replicated. For example, you may think that customers who pay a certain amount of tax would be good customers, but how much tax someone pays is hard to find and therefore that segment – while perhaps valid – is not reachable cost-effectively.

4 Are the segments stable? You might identify a segment, but if that segment is likely to disappear tomorrow then it's not that useful long term.

5 Are the segments profitable or valuable? Time will often tell with this one, but whatever the results the insights are useful. If a segment turns out not to be profitable then you can stop marketing to that segment and save money, or do greater analysis on the segment to identify a sub-segment that is profitable.

6 Are the segments relevant? You may identify a segment that looks promising, but if that segment doesn't fit with your brand or strategy then it's probably best to focus your attention elsewhere.

Practical example

A greeting card retailer wants to engage in more marketing to attract people to his shop. He starts by making a note of his customers – are they mainly male or female, how old are they, and when they purchase something he asks the customer for their postcode. This data allows him to build a rudimentary picture of his current customers.

Even with this postcode data there are now tools that allow you to extract a significant amount of additional data about that customer based on their postcode.

By building up even a basic picture of current customers the car retailer can then add new data sets such as Facebook 'likes' which can again provide even greater insight into interests, preferences, etc., which can then be used to direct targeted marketing campaigns.

A study conducted by researchers at Cambridge University and Microsoft Research Labs showed how the patterns of Facebook 'likes' can be enough to predict a range of often very personal attributes such as religious beliefs, political views, sexual orientation or how much alcohol we drink. Many of these insights can obviously be very useful for marketers. Albeit a little controversial!

Of course, if the greeting card retailer also sells online then a lot of data about his customers will also be readily available for analysis. Plus, he is able to see where his online customers are coming from, which can also help in appreciating who they are and into what segment they fall.

Tips and traps

It is possible to take segmentation too far and seek to split your customer base down into increasingly smaller sub-groups. This is not always useful. The key is to establish some clusters within your market that seem to behave and buy in similar ·

patterns, figure out what those patterns are and use that insight to position offers to those individuals so as to meet their needs while increasing revenue.

Further reading and references

To learn more about customer segmentation analytics see for example:

- Tsiptsis, K. and Chorianopoulos, A. (2010) *Data Mining Techniques in CRM: Inside Customer Segmentation*, 1st edition, Hoboken, NJ: Wiley
- http://www2.microstrategy.com/download/files/Solutions/byDepartment/CRM/Customer_Segmentation.pdf
- https://www.statsoft.com/Textbook/Customer-Segmentation
- http://www.bain.com/publications/articles/management-tools-customer-segmentation.aspx
- http://www.mbaknol.com/marketing-management/customer-segmentation-analysis/
- http://researchaccess.com/2010/08/customer-segmentation-an-overview/
- http://smallbusiness.chron.com/examples-market-segmentation-14403.html
- http://www.segmentationstudyguide.com/business-segmentation/business-market-segmentation-examples/
- http://www.infoentrepreneurs.org/en/guides/segment-your-customers
- http://www.optimove.com/learning-center/customer-segmentation

Sales channel analytics

46

What is it?

Sales channel analytics looks at all the various ways that you distribute your products to your market to see which channels are the most effective.

There are many different way to sell to customers: businesses may have retail stores, they may use re-sellers or agents, they may sell direct online. It is important to know what sales channels yield the most sales and also the quality of the sales that comes from each sales channel so that you can make the best use of your resources.

Why does it matter?

Sales channel analytics matters because unless you know how your sales are made and what channels are most profitable then you may be wasting time and money on sales channels that don't work or that generate lower-value customers.

This type of analytics allows you to focus on the sales channels that generate the most profit and reach the highest-value customers. Plus, you can also establish channel margins. Each sales channel has associated costs which need to be factored into the decision-making process. For example, running a direct sales force is considerably more expensive than running a website. Plus, it's not just about how many products you sell and how many new customers you acquire; it's also about the quality of those customers and their relative profitability. Sales channel analytics can help you to identify high-quality, profitable customers.

When do I use it?

It's just smart business to know which of your sales channels are producing what result. If you make a habit of engaging in sales channel analytics regularly – at least every year – then you can also establish the channel trend, i.e. is the sales channel remaining constant, growing or is its effectiveness diminishing over time?

You will also be able to spot trends so you can capitalise on changing buying behaviour. You may find, for example, that more and more people are choosing to purchase your products online or on the go. It would therefore make sense to spend any investment you may wish to make on perhaps designing a shopping app for Smartphones to help your customers buy more easily rather than recruit another salesperson.

What business questions is it helping me to answer?

Sales channel analytics help you answer business questions such as:

- Which sales channel generates the most sales?
- Which sales channel generates the most new customers?
- Do those results change for various customer segments?
- Which sales channel is the most profitable?

How do I use it?

First you need to identify all the sales channels that you currently use or could use. This might include online sales channels, be that your own website or other retailer sites that you plug into, direct sales, retail stores or third party sellers.

Sales channel analytics then looks at all the current sales and where they came from. So each sale is attributed to one of the sales channels. By then subtracting the relevant cost of sales for each channel you are able to ascertain which are the most profitable and which channel attracts the highest-value customers.

Obviously this is incredibly important to know because it can impact long-term strategy and how the business develops and grows in the future. Optimising sales channel mix can have a profound impact on the bottom line.

Practical example

A winemaker may sell their wine a number of different ways: they may have a shop on the premises of the vineyard, where customers can see the process and buy the product; they may operate a mail order business; they may provide their wine to a larger wine business; or they may have their own website where customers can buy their wine direct. The winemaker will also have a number of sales representatives who seek to sell the wine direct to restaurants, supermarkets and suitable specialty shops.

Sales channel analysis may indicate that the margin for sales in the online shop are the highest. But the number of sales is fewest via the shop. It's worth doing but it's not enough to sustain the business. The most sales come from the larger wine business, but they also have the smallest margins as the winemaker needs to pay that business a commission. However, it's also worth doing – especially if they can then convert that customer to their own mail order business.

Sales channel analytics makes it possible to gather these insights and tailor your approach accordingly.

Tips and traps

In the same way that you might not know how often your customer was exposed to another marketing channel, you don't always know if the customer was exposed to a different sales channel. In other words, a customer may decide to buy online but they may already have been 'sold' by a direct sales person several months earlier or seen your product in a shop but decided to buy online anyway. In this case the online channel gets the credit for the sale, but actually it was the shop or the sales-person that did most of the work. This anomaly can distort the figures.

Further reading and references

For further insight into sales channel analytics see for example:

- Dent, J. (2011) *Distribution Channels: Understanding and Managing Channels to Market*, 2nd edition, London: Kogan Page
- http://www.mckinsey.com/client_service/marketing_and_sales/expertise/sales_and_channel_management
- http://www.academia.edu/2741798/Managing_sales_return_in_dual_sales_channel_An_analysis_of_its_product_substitution

47

Web analytics

What is it?

Web analytics is the process of analysing online behaviour so as to optimise website use and increase engagement and sales.

There are two types of web analytics – off-site and on-site. Off-site web analytics looks at what is happening on the internet as a whole and includes the measurement of a product or service's potential audience, competition and online trends. On-site web analytics is the analysis of your own website. This includes collecting data on how many people visited the site, where they came from, how long they stayed, how they navigated the site and whether the visit resulted in a sale. Off-site web analytics is useful for assessing the market and opportunity whereas on-site is useful for measuring commercial results.

Why does it matter?

Web analytics matters because online sales in just about every industry are increasing. More and more people are connected to the internet via a computer, tablet or Smartphone, which creates a significant online opportunity for just about every business. Most companies have a website but having one is not enough; you need to know how effective it is. Web analytics can tell you. If the results show that your website is not performing then it is also fairly easy and quick to conduct market research with your customers to either ask them what they want or test some changes to see what elevates performance. For example, you could test new landing pages on your site to see which one attracts more visitors or leads to more sales.

Plus web analytics is an incredibly cost effective and immediate way to test marketing ideas. Traditionally, when using direct marketing for example a campaign may include a number of different versions to see which version performs the best. That version may then be used as the control and new campaigns would test against that approach to see if response rates could be improved. Now marketers can test campaigns, offers, pricing or headlines online prior to a TV, print or direct marketing campaign to identify the best performers before spending all the money in production.

When do I use it?

It's probably enough to conduct off-site web analytics once a year unless you operate in a particularly volatile market. The off-site analytics helps to measure trends in your industry so you can be alerted of changes in plenty of time to adapt your offering.

On-site web analytics should be conducted constantly so you know how many visitors you are attracting to your website and what they are doing once they get there.

It can also be beneficial to test various offers and marketing campaigns online before they go live on other more expensive media. For example, you could test your TV ad online to gauge response. Although the costs are still applicable for making the ad, most of the real cost is spent airing the advert on TV – being able to predict response ahead of that investment is very useful.

What business questions is it helping me to answer?

Web analytics help you answer business questions such as:

- How many people are visiting our website?
- Who are the visitors to our website?
- How do visitors find our website?
- What search terms do people use to find our website?
- What pages are they visiting?
- Are there any pages that are not being used that could be deleted?
- How long do visitors stay on the site?
- What is the conversion rate from visitors to sales?
- What are the online trends in my industry?

How do I use it?

There are many web analytics tools and service providers, although Google analytics is probably the front-runner. What's brilliant about these tools is that you just have to set up what you want to measure and asses and the tool will do all the work for you.

So while you could easily create your own tracking tools and embed them into your website, for example, it just doesn't make sense anymore. The tools are already available and most of them are also free so wasting time and money re-inventing an already very accurate and sophisticated wheel is not a good use of your resources.

There are also tools such as CrazyEgg which shows you what parts of your website are 'hot', 'warm' or 'cold'. Hot and warm areas of the site indicate where customers are visiting and staying. Cold areas are where there is no traffic or the customer quickly leaves. These insights can therefore help you to refine your online presence and give your customers more of what they demonstrate they want and less of what they demonstrate they don't want.

Practical example

As you might expect online search engine Yahoo! Inc uses web analytics to impact revenue and profit. As one of the most popular search engines in the world Yahoo! receives millions of hits to its home page every hour. As a result, they have access to a massive amount of data that allows them to test new hypothesis or assumptions very quickly. For example, Yahoo! wanted to know whether alterations to their home page would change visitor behaviour and if so how.

They devised an experiment where they randomly assigned several hundred thousand users to an experimental group, leaving the rest as the control group. This allowed them to establish whether or not the changes to the home page resulted in the anticipated or desired behaviour change or not. The insights gained from this experiment allowed them to optimise their offerings to all users and therefore enhance revenues and profits. Plus the results of these experiments were often visible within minutes, making them an extremely dynamic tool for shaping company strategy and direction. The speed of accurate feedback together with minimal disruption and low cost mean Yahoo! typically runs about 20 experiments of this type at any given time.

As well as being cost-effective and immediate, Yahoo! also benefit because they are able to cut out all the lengthy discussions about website design and layout because it's the evidence-based results that drive behaviour and strategic direction and not personal preference, consensus or even a dominant opinion.

Tips and traps

The real value of web analytics emerges if you continue to do it and can see how your online performance is changing over time. It is also a fantastic way to run market research without running market research. If you try something online – if it doesn't work you change it. There is nothing printed or distributed, no man power on the streets asking questions – all you need to do is try something, assess the response and try something else.

Plus be sure to check out your competitor's website too and compare your web performance to your competition. And there are a range of ways to do this (see references.)

The biggest online trap is building a website and leaving it. If you don't run analytics you won't know if it's working or not. And even if it does work if you don't run analytics you won't know why, so you may be even more reluctant to change it because you won't know why it's working. Web analytics is absolutely essential in the commercial online world.

Further reading and references

For further insight into how web analytics can help your business see for example:

- Kaushik, A. (2009) *Web Analytics 2.0: The Art of Online Accountability and Science of Customer Centricity*, 1st edition, Hoboken, NJ: Sybex
- Clifton, B. (2012) *Advanced Web Metrics with Google Analytics*, 3rd edition, Hoboken, NJ: Sybex
- Ellis, B. (2014) *Real-Time Analytics: Techniques to Analyse and Visualize Streaming Data*, 1st edition, Hoboken, NJ: Wiley
- http://www.inc.com/guides/12/2010/11-best-web-analytics-tools.html
- http://www.google.co.uk/analytics/
- http://www.forbes.com/sites/kaviguppta/2014/10/27/hey-chartbeat-heres-how-web-analytics-needs-to-change/
- http://www.usability.gov/what-and-why/web-analytics.html
- http://www.huffingtonpost.com/penny-c-sansevieri/how-to-analyze-your-websi_b_1806389.html
- http://www.kaushik.net/avinash/beginners-guide-web-data-analysis-ten-steps-tips-best-practices/
- http://www.orbitmedia.com/blog/website-competitive-analysis-tools/
- http://www.quicksprout.com/2013/12/11/how-to-analyze-your-competition-in-less-than-60-seconds/

48

Social media analytics

What is it?

Social media analytics is the process of gathering and analysing data from social media. The rise of social media has created a rich vein of data from individuals who are customers or potential customers. Most people have a Smartphone and will share their thoughts and feelings regularly via Facebook, Twitter or many of the other social media platforms. This data can then be assessed to find out what people are saying about your product, service, brand or company.

Why does it matter?

Social media analytics matters because it offers you an almost real-time glimpse into what your customers or potential customers think and feel about your business.

These insights can be used to increase revenue by tapping into unmet customer needs (Chapter 34), reduce customer service costs and highlight customer service issues that cause loss of business or reputation. They can also be used by product development to gain real-world feedback on products and services. Often in focus groups (Chapter 21) people will tell you what they think you want to hear or will tone down their dissatisfaction because they don't want to 'appear rude'. Social media analytics can give you the real unadulterated view – for better or for worse. Whether good or bad, the truth allows you to take action and improve performance or improve on the product in a way that will resonate with your customers.

Plus, if you don't know what people are saying about your company or products, you can't step in to solve the issue or turn an unhappy customer into a raving fan.

When do I use it?

Social media is a permanent and almost constant feature in millions of people's lives. Those millions of people are posting their opinion on social media via their Smartphones and tablets constantly, therefore you should be analysing what's being said constantly.

Many big businesses have social media command centres that are monitoring their products, services and brands constantly and using those insights to inform decision making and direct strategy. But it's not just for big business – social media analytics is essential for all businesses, large and small.

What business questions is it helping me to answer?

Social media analytics helps you answer business questions such as:

- What are our customers saying about the company/brand/product?
- Are our customers satisfied with their interaction with our business or not?
- Are there any problems or issues being raised by our customers on social media that we can solve?
- If you are engaging in social media – who is reading your posts?
- How many followers do you have on Twitter or LinkedIn, or how many likes do you have on Facebook?

How do I use it?

Social media analytics essentially gathers text data from social media posts and blogs and that data is then mined (Chapter 6) for commercially relevant insights.

This can include text analytics (Chapter 8) and sentiment analysis (Chapter 9). Sentiment analysis is one of the most common social media analytic tools as it determines whether customers or potential customers see your brand, product or service positively or negatively, and these trends can aid decision making.

You should know the trends around your product or service every week. There are many tools available to help you achieve this such as Google Social Analytics, SumAll, Facebook Insights and Twitter Analytics.

Practical example

Since 2010 sports drink company Gatorade have operated a social media command centre inside its Chicago HQ. Monitoring their brand in real time across social media platforms and the blogosphere has proved invaluable to the company.

Monitoring their 'Gatorade has evolved' campaign, which featured a song by rap artist David Banner, they were able to see that the song was being heavily discussed on social media. Within 24 hours, they had worked with Banner to put out a full-length version of the song and distribute it to Gatorade followers and fans on Twitter and Facebook, respectively. The company is also using the insights from the social media command centre to optimise landing pages and ensure followers are being sent to the top-performing pages. As an example, the company says it's been able to increase engagement with its product education (mostly video) by 250 per cent and reduce its exit rate from 25 to 9 per cent.[1]

Tips and traps

The real power of social media analytics is its real-time immediate nature. If you can spot unhappy customers as soon as they indicate their frustration then you have an opportunity to turn that situation around and create a loyal customer. That means you need to use it and look at it frequently because the 'shelf life' of the insights are short or potentially short. In addition you need to empower your customer service team to engage with your customers quickly to solve issues.

The biggest trap for social media analytics is to become obsessed with numbers – how many followers or how many Facebook 'likes' you have, rather than looking more closely to see how many of those followers are customers and how to engage the audience to encourage more people to purchase your products or services.

Further reading and references

To learn more about social media analytics see for example:

- Sponder, M. (2013) *Social Media Analytics: Effective Tools for Building, Interpreting, and Using Metrics*, New York: McGraw-Hill
- Russell, M.A. (2013) *Mining the Social Web: Data Mining Facebook, Twitter, LinkedIn, Google+, GitHub, and More*, 2nd edition, Sebastopol, CA: O'Reilly Media
- Danneman, N. and Heimann, R. (2014) *Social Media Mining with R*, Birmingham, UK: Packt Publishing
- http://www.sas.com/en_us/software/customer-intelligence/social-media-analytics.html
- http://venturebeat.com/2013/12/20/top-10-social-media-analytics-tools-the-venturebeat-index/
- http://mashable.com/2012/02/09/social-media-analytics-spreadsheets/

---

[1] Ostrow, A. (2010) 'Inside Gatorade's Social Media Command Center Mashable', http://mashable.com/2010/06/15/gatorade-social-media-mission-control/

- http://www.salesforce.com/uk/socialsuccess/social-media-how-to-guides/social-media-analytics-guide-metrics-tools.jsp
- http://www.goldbachinteractive.com/current-news/technical-papers/social-media-monitoring-how-it-s-done
- http://www.entrepreneur.com/article/239029
- http://www.razorsocial.com/social-media-analytics-tools

49 Customer engagement analytics

What is it?

Customer engagement analytics is a highly evolving field at the moment where businesses are trying to map the entire customer interactive journey on- and offline. In essence it is the process of assessing how well (or otherwise) you engage your customers with your products, services or brand through these various interactions.

Engagement is a subjective term, but thankfully research firm Gallup has simplified the various levels of engagement. Based on answers to just 11 questions Gallup have categorised customer engagement according to four levels:

- **Fully engaged customers** – those who are emotionally attached and rationally loyal to your business. These are your most valuable customers.
- **Engaged customers** – those who are beginning to feel the stirrings of emotional engagement. These customers are ripe for development and could relatively easily be pushed up to fully engaged.
- **Disengaged customers** – those who are emotionally and rationally neutral. These customers are also ripe for development because they are neutral so could be swayed upwards (or pushed downwards).
- **Actively disengaged customers** – those who are emotionally detached and actively antagonistic. These customers pose a serious threat to your business – especially in the age of the internet and social media.

Customer engagement analytics can help you figure out how many of each you have, what to do about it and what you need to do in the future to ensure more fully engaged customers and less actively disengaged customers.

Why does it matter?

Customer engagement matters because business is notoriously bad at it and yet it impacts bottom line results. When customers want to speak to you and get passed around several departments, having to explain the situation all over again to each department, this can be infuriating for customers. Often businesses end up operating various different systems that don't communicate with each other and one part of the business will not necessarily know what another part is doing. This often happens in banking. And being able, therefore, to know all the customer interactions and map the journey a customer has with you is becoming increasingly important.

Not least because it has been discovered that customer satisfaction is not the predictor of behaviour that many companies once assumed it was. The argument has always been that satisfied customers = loyal customers = profit. Unfortunately in the modern world of multiple options and constant deals, whether a customer is satisfied is not necessarily enough to keep them as a customer.

For example, Xerox found that more than a quarter of their customers defected at the end of their contract despite describing themselves as 'satisfied' customers. Further analysis by Xerox found that there were strong correlations between genuine loyalty and customer longevity and whether customers described themselves as 'very satisfied'. When those 'very satisfied' customers were pressed further to explain their satisfaction it almost always came down to their engagement or the nature of their perceived relationship with Xerox.

Gallup's research data has also backed up this argument. Collected from almost three million customers in 16 major industries across 53 countries over a four-year period their research revealed that fully engaged customers deliver, on average, 23 per cent more in terms of profitability, share of wallet, revenue and relationship growth than the average customer. Actively disengaged customers represent a 13 per cent discount in those same measures. Companies that have high engagement have outperformed their competitors by 26 per cent in gross margin and 85 per cent in sales growth, and their customers buy more, spend more, return more often and stay longer. Customer engagement is the key to keeping customers, not necessarily satisfaction – so measuring engagement really matters.

When do I use it?

You would be wise to conduct customer engagement analytics at least every six months so that you can establish whether the trend is stable, positive or negative. The earlier you know of any problems that could be affecting customer engagement the faster you can potentially solve those problems and maintain high levels of customer engagement.

It is also especially useful and relevant if you are making any changes to your product or service or introducing new systems that will impact the customer experience.

What business questions is it helping me to answer?

Customer engagement analytics helps you answer business questions such as:

- How engaged are our customers with our products, services or brand?
- How are our customers interacting with us?
- Can everyone in the business appreciate the entire journey or do they just see their part?
- Are our customers interacting with us on social media?

How do I use it?

Historical customer engagement can be measured via a survey (Chapters 19 and 20) to gauge customer engagement. Social media analytics can also be used to measure engagement (Chapter 48).

That said, every company needs to create their own model for what 'engagement' is in their context. There are specialist companies that can help you to create your own customer engagement model and there are also many tools that can turn the data from places like Google Analytics into a customer engagement score. These scores can then help you to predict engagement which can in turn direct decision making and strategy.

Practical example

US-based Rent-A-Car deliberately moved away from satisfaction analysis to a self-designed analysis tool called the Enterprise Service Quality Index (ESQi). The reason for this move was that, like Xerox, internal research had demonstrated that customers who stated they were 'completely satisfied' on a five-point scale from 'completely satisfied' to 'completely dissatisfied' were three times more likely to return as a customer and recommend Rent-A-Car to others.

Customer engagement analytics found that these customers value the relationship with Enterprise Rent-A-Car and so can be described as 'engaged'. As a result of this analysis all Rent-A-Car offices are only measured against how many of their customers are 'completely satisfied'. Focusing their attention to ensure that as many customers as possible state they are 'completely satisfied' with their Rent-A-Car experience has increased results. Knowing that 'satisfied' alone is not good enough and that 'satisfied' does not result in repeat business and increased revenue has allowed the company to deliver better than expected service.

Tips and traps

You can't please all of the people all of the time, but customer engagement analytics can help to identify what aspects of your product or service are most valued so you can constantly improve your offering and maintain valuable connections to your customers.

Don't expect to find the perfect model straight up. Decide on a model that seems to make sense to your business and your customers and run with it. You may then need to fine tune it as you use it, but that process is made much easier if you get into action instead of getting stuck because 'the model isn't perfect'.

Further reading and references

For further insight into customer engagement analytics see for example:

- Paharia, R. (2013) *Loyalty 3.0: How to Revolutionize Customer and Employee Engagement with Big Data and Gamification*, New York: McGraw-Hill
- Sauro, J. (2015) *Customer Analytics For Dummies*, Hoboken, NJ: Wiley
- http://www.nice.com/customer-engagement-analytics
- http://www.sap.com/pc/tech/in-memory-computing-hana/software/customer-engagement-analytics/index.html
- https://hbr.org/resources/pdfs/comm/sap/18764_HBR_SAP_Telcom_July_14.pdf
- http://www.evergage.com/blog/customer-engagement-analytics-5-steps-success/
- http://www.sas.com/en_us/news/press-releases/2014/december/telco-sma-swisscom.html

50 Customer churn analytics

What is it?

Customer churn analytics is the process of assessing how many customers you are losing over the course of a year. Often we are so focused on getting new customers that we don't realise how many existing customers are leaving – customer churn analytics can help answer those questions.

Winning customers is one challenge, but keeping them is just as important and your customer churn can therefore be a powerful indicator of future financial performance. Obviously, if you are losing more customers than you are gaining then you are going to run into trouble.

Customer churn analytics also allows you to predict customer churn in the future and take evasive action before you lose those customers.

Why does it matter?

Customer churn analytics matters because keeping your existing customers is always much easier and cheaper than trying to find new customers.

Once a customer has bought from you once, they are much more likely to buy from you again because they have made the initial buying decision. The first purchase is always the hardest as the customer decides between competing products and brands. It is just as important to keep customers as it is to secure them in the first place because it's always considerably easier to sell to that customer again, up-sell them to a more expensive product or cross-sell them a different product from your range. Customer churn analytics therefore ensures that you don't take your eye off the ball and retain as many as possible moving forward.

When do I use it?

Again this depends on your industry and the average lifetime value of your customer (Chapter 44). It is best to put in a regular data stream to ensure you get insights on a monthly basis.

It also depends on how proactive you are willing to be in order to reduce churn. If, for example, you recognise that customer churn represents a significant opportunity and you operate in a very competitive industry then you may be motivated to reduce this rate as much as you can, in which case you should run this analysis monthly and monitor the trends. These insights also give you information so you can assess what is causing the churn and test approaches to stop it.

What business questions is it helping me to answer?

Customer churn analytics helps you answer business questions such as:

- How many customers do I lose?
- Which customers are leaving?
- Are their trends in the churn, i.e. do they leave more at certain times?

How do I use it?

Customer churn can be assessed using key performance indicators (KPI) such as customer retention rate (CRR) and customer turnover rate (CTR). This data, however, will only tell you what's happening in the past.

Adding historical KPI data to new data sets such as campaign data, sales data or social media text data can allow you to predict customer churn. For example, you could run text analytics (Chapter 8) on customer forums, social media feeds and Twitter posts to help you predict who is thinking about leaving or about to leave so you can intervene before they do. You can also run regression analysis (Chapter 7) to help identify what factors are causing the churn so you can improve those areas or offer a certain segment of your market a slightly different offer to keep them.

Practical example

A telecom company I was working with had a high customer churn. The telecom market is notorious for customer churn and more and more people are happy to swap providers and upgrade their phone to get a better deal. Using customer churn analytics alongside some of the new data sets allowed the telecom company to create a predictive model to better help them understand their customers' behaviour.

Although they were privy to a vast amount of data, they had never looked at how people called each other. They didn't, for example, know whether their customers made mainly inbound or mainly outbound calls. They didn't know how long they spoke for or what times of the day were most popular. By mining that data (Chapter 6) and applying analytics such as customer churn analytics they found that one particular calling pattern was much more likely to churn than all the rest.

This information was extremely valuable to the company because they had not previously been able to identify a 'type' of customer that was more likely to leave. This insight allowed them to finally identify those customers most likely to leave so they could target that segment of the market with special offers and deals that would entice them to stay. As a result they decreased churn and increased revenue.

Tips and traps

Pay particular attention to how you count customers and set that as a company-wide benchmark for the future. If you don't, then different departments may class a customer differently, which can easily pollute the data and render the analysis invalid. For example, if a customer is a customer of more than one product of yours, are they counted for each product or only once? If there is more than one customer from one household, are they counted as individual customers or one household? Whatever you decide, make it a rule in the business so that calculations are meaningful and comparable moving forward. Also, clearly define what 'lost' means. When is a customer no longer a customer? For ongoing regular purchases like a mobile phone contract that may be simple, but if your product or service is not ongoing, is a customer considered 'lost' after they haven't bought from you in six months, a year, three years? Again you need to define this and make it a company-wide standard.

Also, customer churn is not always a bad thing. Sometimes there are customers that you might be quite fortunate to lose. This is why customer lifetime value (Chapter 44) and customer profitability (Chapter 29) are so important. You need to know who your high-value, profitable customers are and who your low-value, unprofitable customers are so you can reduce churn in the right segment. Clearly, if you are experiencing high churn in a customer segment that actually costs you money to service then that is a good result not a bad one. By knowing which is which you can also actively seek churn by pricing the costly customers out of the business so they go and lose money for your competitors.

Further reading and references

To understand more about customer churn analytics see for example:

- Sauro, J. (2015) *Customer Analytics For Dummies*, Hoboken, NJ: Wiley
- Klepac, G. and Kopal, R. (2014) *Developing Churn Models Using Data Mining Techniques and Social Network Analysis*, Hershey, PA: IGI Publishing
- http://www.statsoft.com/Solutions/Financial/Churn-Analysis
- http://www.cmo.com.au/article/458724/how_predictive_analytics_tackling_customer_attrition_american_express/
- http://www.sas.com/success/pdf/edfenergy-churn.pdf

Customer acquisition analytics

51

What is it?

Customer acquisition analytics seeks to establish how effective you are at acquiring new customers, including how effective you are at pinching customers from your competitors.

This type of analysis can help assess how successful acquisition has been in the past and also predict the future so you can ensure your sales and marketing initiatives are cost-effective and productive.

Why does it matter?

Customer acquisition analytics matters because if you don't have enough customers your business will fail. If you are spending too much money acquiring those customers your business will fail. And if you don't know how much you are spending then you can't make changes to the process to ensure profitability as early as possible.

The key function of marketing is to let people know about your business, brand, products or services, but customer acquisition analytics looks at how successful you then are in turning that awareness into a sale and actually acquiring a customer. This type of analytics looks at the whole journey that a prospect goes through prior to the close of the sale, and works out if that process works as well as possible.

When do I use it?

You need to know where if anywhere your customer acquisition processes might fall down. For example, is it the marketing? Is it the product quality? Is it the delivery time? Is it the sales processes? Perhaps placing the order is too complicated or asks for too much information. As a result, you should conduct this type of analysis at least every year or whenever something changes in the acquisition process.

For example, you may use radio advertising very effectively and your customer acquisition costs may be quite low. However, if the radio advertising goes up in price or the effectiveness begins to drop you need to know about that as soon as possible, not six months after you've been losing money on radio advertising.

What business questions is it helping me to answer?

Customer acquisition analytics helps you answer business questions such as:

- How successful is my marketing department at attracting new customers?
- How successful are my sales department at converting initial interest or leads into a paying customer?
- How much does it cost to generate those leads in the first place?
- Are there any problems in the buying process that are putting prospective customers off making the final purchase?

How do I use it?

There are a number of metrics that can help to establish historic data on acquisition. For example, you can use the cost per lead (CPL) key performance indicator. As the name would suggest, cost per lead works out how much it costs to attract each potential customer to your product offering, and it is a powerful leading indicator of likely future revenue. The assumption is that if you can attract potential customers cost-effectively then sales in the future will be strong.

That said, not all leads are equal so to make this metric more accurate and indicative of future performance you need to calculate cost per qualified lead. A qualified lead is someone who is definitely in the market for what you are selling and is at least in principle ready to buy. Another useful metric to assess past results is the customer conversion rate (CCR). This metric looks at how successful you are at converting leads, qualified or otherwise, into paying customers.

If you acquire new customers online there is also a wealth of data that can then help you to analyse the entire customer journey. You can track what parts of the website they visit, what they read and visit, all the way up to the point of sale. This means that you know when a customer places a product in their shopping basket on your website but don't buy and at what stage in the process they drop out. Customer acquisition analytics looks to uncover why. For example, if you discover that a high number of people reject the purchase because they have to first register and add loads of personal data then you could revise the registration process to only ask for the absolutely necessary information. This sort of insight is also possible in the offline world using camera and sensor data (Chapter 26), although it's not so easy.

There is also a great deal of data around acquisition on review sites or social media. For example, if people are complaining about the time it takes for your business to deliver your products or complaining about the standard of the packaging when it did arrive, then these insights should be used to assess what's going wrong and how you can quickly improve.

Practical example

Say you operate a car dealership for BMW. All the marketing for BMW will be done centrally. The purpose of that marketing is to raise awareness and drive potential local customers into your dealership. But do you know how successful you are at then converting that interest into sales?

You could install cameras at the dealership so that you know how many people visit the site. Using video analytics (Chapter 11) you identify how long each salesperson spends with each client and whether certain salespeople consistently outperform the rest. You could also track what people are saying about your dealership online to identify if there are any weaknesses in the acquisition process that can be solved.

Tips and traps

When calculating cost per lead and cost per qualified lead calculate them separately for each marketing initiative or campaign you execute. This will help you make better decisions and give you a much clearer picture of what is working and what is not. If you try to calculate cost per lead or cost per qualified lead across multiple initiatives then there are too many variables that could skew the result and you won't get very meaningful data.

Further reading and references

To find out more about customer acquisition analytics see for example:

- Putler, D.S. and Krider, R.E. (2012) *Customer and Business Analytics: Applied Data Mining for Business Decision Making Using R*, Hove: CRC Press

- Sauro, J. (2015) *Customer Analytics For Dummies*, Hoboken, NJ: Wiley

- http://online-behaviour.com/analytics/customer-acquisition-analysis

[PART SIX]

Employee analytics

Capability analytics

52

What is it?

Capability analytics is a talent management process that allows you to identify the capabilities or core competencies you want and need in your business. Once you know what those capabilities are you can then analyse your current staff members to see if you have any capability gaps.

Knowing what skills you need and what you already have in your business via a rigorous analytics process can alert you to issues you may not have been aware of so you can retrain or support individuals to close those gaps more effectively.

Why does it matter?

Capability analytics matters because the success of your business depends on the level of expertise and skill of your workforce. Too often we hire new employees without really knowing exactly what skills we already have and what additional skills we need. As a result we hire based on gut instinct or what is written on a CV, or how well or otherwise someone comes across in interview. There may be a laundry list of 'ideal candidate characteristics', but they are often generic personality issues such as 'honesty' and 'integrity' rather than 'capability in X software', etc.

When these new recruits join the business you may hope that they will fit in and work well with the existing team, but if you are unsure exactly what capability you expect them to bring to the table beyond being another pair of hands then you will almost certainly be disappointed with the appointment. Capability analytics helps to avoid this scenario so that you know exactly what you need, what you have and what additional capabilities you may need to recruit to close the gap. Or what additional training you need to provide those that are already in the business to close that gap.

This is especially important if your business, industry or market is changing quickly.

When do I use it?

It is always wise to conduct capability analytics at least once a year and certainly before every significant or important appointment. For those already in the business, capability analytics can slot into the annual performance review to inform ongoing training and improvement initiatives.

Knowing who can do what can also allow you to move people around the business, providing additional training or support to those who could adapt to a new role or position. Just because someone is doing one job now does not mean they don't have the capability to do another. But you won't know what someone is fully capable of unless you conduct capability analytics.

It is also sensible to run capability analytics if your business is changing and moving into a new area or slightly different direction that will require additional or different capabilities.

What business questions is it helping me to answer?

Capability analytics helps you answer business questions such as:

- What are our core competencies in the business?
- What capabilities do our key members of staff possess?
- What capabilities will the business need moving forward?
- Is there a shortfall between what we have and what we need?

How do I use it?

Capability analytics can be conducted via questionnaire (Chapters 19 and 20) and by interview (Chapter 22) of the individual being assessed and also the people who work with them closely. It is often easier to acknowledge and appreciate someone else's capabilities than it is to see our own.

Once you know what capabilities you have and what capabilities you need you can then create a competency framework for your business. Often this can mean that you ask people to re-apply for their jobs but it doesn't have to be so alarming for employees. If highlighted early enough, through capability analytics the move to more relevant and more needed skills can simply become part of the ongoing employee training and annual performance reviews.

Practical example

Say you are an IT manufacturer. The speed of change in the IT industry both in terms of the technological capabilities of the machines we use and buying behaviour means that it's a highly volatile industry.

Just a decade ago you were riding high, manufacturing large mainframe computers as well as smaller machines for the personal use market. But business doesn't really want large mainframes any more. The advent of cloud computing has massively changed the market. By conducting detailed capability analytics you realise that the capabilities that made you a dominant force last decade will render you obsolete in the next.

To stem this potentially disastrous outcome you create a competency framework for your business outlining specific and generic capabilities. For example, you might appreciate that everyone in the business needs to improve their 'customer focus' competency. In addition you might appreciate that within your specialist IT centres there needs to be a new competency created around 'Big Data', which will require Hadoop skills and cloud computing skills that don't currently exist in the business. This competency framework therefore directs HR intervention so that they can source appropriate training and/or recruit new employees to kick start the skill shift.

Tips and traps

Capabilities are not just about qualifications and skills; they can also include capabilities that may not be formally recognised. For example, you may know that a certain member of your team is extremely good at developing and maintaining relationships. This is a capability even though there is no certificate to prove the ability.

Don't throw the baby out with the bathwater. Just because you have employees that don't quite cover all the capabilities you need or will need in the future does not mean you need to get rid of them and find others. There is more to success in the workplace than capability. Fit in the team, cultural fit and existing relationships are also very important. It is often much easier to keep all that and retrain to create the capability than find the capability and hope that individual then fits into the culture or team.

Further reading and references

For further insight into capability analytics see for example:

- Fitz-enz, J. and Mattoxx, J. (2014) *Predictive Analytics for Human Resources*, Hoboken, NJ: Wiley
- Kinley, N. and Ben-Hur, S. (2013) *Talent Intelligence: What You Need to Know to Identify and Measure Talent*, 1st edition, San Francisco, CA: Jossey-Bass

53

Capacity analytics

What is it?

Capacity analytics seeks to establish how operationally efficient individual employees are.

Taking into account administration time, travel time, etc., a consultant may have 30 potential 'billable hours' per week and capacity analytics would determine how many of those 30 potential billable hours are actually billed out to clients and, therefore, how much additional capacity he or she still has for more work.

Why does it matter?

Capacity analytics matters because it affects revenue.

If you don't know what your people are doing and how many billable hours they are actually billing for then you can't manage that employee capacity more appropriately. If one consultant is at full capacity then he or she should not be expected to pick up the slack with the new client. If another consultant is spending too much time on administration then he or she is not productive or profitable.

When do I use it?

It is wise to measure capacity every six months or at least every year. People are people, not machines, so an individual's capacity will fluctuate throughout the year based on a variety of factors.

These peaks and troughs of productivity are normal. However, capacity analytics can help to alert you to negative or worrying productivity trends. This analysis allows you to then step in with additional training or support to help the individual get back on track before they become too demoralised or negative.

What business questions is it helping me to answer?

Capacity analytics helps you answer business questions such as:

- How effectively do we employ our people?
- To what extent do we have spare capacity in our company?
- To what extent do we overstretch out people?

How do I use it?

As long as you have a system that tracks data on how people spend their time you can use this data to establish capacity levels. The data can come from time-tracking systems (where people clock in and out) or from sensors (see Chapter 26). Some companies even use RFID (radio frequency identification) sensors in name badges to track where employees are, which allows them to automatically assign what people are doing – e.g. by pulling in data on what department they are in, which office they are in, what machine they are working on, etc.

This data can then pulled into analysis software or even tools such as Microsoft Excel for analysis.

Practical example

Say you are a software engineering company and you have 20 software engineers working in your business. Capacity analytics will allow you to track how much time they actually spend coding and how much time they spend doing other work. This ratio can then be tracked over time to ensure the actual time spent (obviously relative to the billable output) on programming is not going down.

It also allows the company to understand how much capacity they have to take on new projects. If everyone is at 100 per cent capacity then taking on any more work is not advisable unless capacity can be increased by, for example, recruiting new staff.

Capacity analytics can also help to identify patterns and trends in employee performance that can then be used to improve recruitment or training and development.

Tips and traps

Capacity analytics can make people very nervous. The idea is not to find out who to whip into greater effort, but rather to identify gaps in capacity that can then be closed to increase profit. Be careful how you position capacity analytics to your people.

Further reading and references

For further insight into capacity analytics see for example:

- http://www-03.ibm.com/software/products/en/capacity-management-analytics/
- http://www.infosys.com/products-and-platforms/information-management-infrastructure/resource-center/Documents/hospital-capacity-analytics.pdf

Employee churn analytics

54

What is it?

Employee churn analytics is the process of assessing your staff turnover rates in the past in an attempt to predict the future.

Your employees are your most important and often most expensive asset. Using analytics to assess capability and hire the right people (Chapter 55) is just part of the process. Then you've got to keep them. Employee churn analytics allows you to plot these trends and predict the future so you can intervene earlier and reduce employee churn.

Why does it matter?

Employee churn analytics matters because hiring employees, training them and then integrating them into the business and getting them up to speed costs time and money. When that investment is lost because too many employees are leaving the business then this can have a detrimental impact on the business.

Plus, high staff turnover can be extremely disruptive to the remaining team members and leads to drops in morale and staff productivity. People always work best when they know and get along with the other people they work with, build up trust and interact with each other – if staff turnover is too high then these beneficial alliances don't get a chance to develop and this can affect revenue.

When do I use it?

Depending on the volatility of your business you should track employee churn analytics every six months or annually. Some businesses have higher staff turnover than others. For example, call centres have notoriously high staff turnover especially compared to more traditional manufacturing.

You need to know the trend – i.e. is there more, less or stable employee churn in your business. If the trend is heading up then this can offer a red flag for further investigation to stabilise turnover or even reduce it further.

What business questions is it helping me to answer?

Employee churn analytics helps you answer business questions such as:

- How satisfied are our employees?
- Which employees are at risk of leaving?
- What is the average tenure for our employees?
- How engaged are our employees?
- What is causing our employees to leave?

How do I use it?

Historical employee churn can be identified through traditional key performance indicators such as the employee satisfaction index (ESI), employee engagement level and staff advocacy score.

In addition, the use of surveys (Chapters 19 and 20) and exit interviews (Chapter 22) can help to gather additional information that can then be mined for greater insights (Chapter 6). Text analytics (Chapter 8) can also be used on that data as well as performance reviews and social media data.

Historical employee churn rates can be useful as a benchmark, but the real gold comes by comparing your business against industry averages, seeking to identify patterns and, perhaps most useful, applying different analytics techniques such as regression (Chapter 7) to understand *why* people are leaving. Once you know why then you can predict employee churn and also, most importantly, take any necessary internal action that would solve the problem and keep employees engaged.

Practical example

Say you operate a knitwear business. You employ people who are highly skilled and they are increasingly difficult to replace if they leave. Recently they have been leaving in greater numbers and you are becoming alarmed so you conduct some employee churn analytics.

You recruit an independent researcher to conduct exit interviews with employees in the last six months. You assume that these employees are being tempted away by the promise of high wages elsewhere. Your brand is strong and you know that employees are proud to work for the company but something is pulling them elsewhere. At least that's what you think.

The exit interview data is inconclusive. Even though the individuals have left, they are smart enough not to want to burn their bridges in a small town with limited employment so they say things like, 'Oh it was time for a change' or 'I just wanted a new challenge'. However, when the researcher looked back at performance appraisal information and introduced social media data a quite different picture emerged. One particular manager on the factory floor was causing bottlenecks and then blaming his team when delivery deadlines were not met. Although you knew he could be a little caustic and blunt you didn't realise the level of upset he was causing. The churn was largely down to this one individual and his negative impact far outweighed his positive impact so he was moved sideways away from direct interaction with your skilled workforce.

Tips and traps

If you are utilising annual surveys to measure your employees then you are almost certainly missing valuable data. What's important is the trend, so instead of getting all your employees to complete a survey once a year, invite a 10th of the workforce to complete the survey every month for 10 months. That way everyone still only completes the survey once a year but you have 10 data points not one and that insight can allow you to make in-time corrections to minimise employee churn.

Also, if you are going to use employee surveys be sure to use the insights they deliver otherwise you run the risk that the surveys without any action will simple disenfranchise your employees still further. When your people feel they are listened to and what they say matters and you are genuinely trying to address the issues they raise, then not only will they continue to complete the surveys – giving you additional ongoing insights – but they are also much more likely to stay and work productively.

Further reading and references

To understand more about employee churn analytics see for example:

- Waber, B. (2013) *People Analytics: How Social Sensing Technology Will Transform Business and What It Tells Us about the Future*, Upper Saddle River, NJ: Pearson FT Press
- http://www.predictiveanalyticsworld.com/patimes/employee-churn-201-calculating-employee-value/
- http://www.talentanalytics.com/wp-content/uploads/2014/12/Talent-Analytics_EmployeeChurn-OReilly-Case-Study.pdf
- http://www.ehow.com/info_8117008_employee-turnover-analysis.html
- http://management.about.com/od/employeemotivation/a/Employee-Turnover.htm
- http://smallbusiness.chron.com/analyze-employee-turnover-rate-10294.html
- http://www.xperthr.co.uk/good-practice-manual/measuring-labour-turnover/115873/

Recruitment channel analytics

What is it?

Recruitment channel analytics is the process of working out where your best employees come from and what recruitment channels are most effective.

There are many ways to recruit employees such as print advertising, adverts in specialist journals or magazines, online recruitment websites and recruitment consultants. Their costs vary wildly and the time required to recruit through these various channels also varies significantly. Knowing which ones are working and which channels are most cost-effective is therefore important for ongoing recruitment.

Traditionally, recruitment success has been measured by simply counting the number of applications delivered or the number of positions filled. Modern recruitment is, however, full of data and while that allows us to track reach, engagement and costs per appropriate candidate, the ultimate measure is how many people are successfully recruited and actually stay with your organisation.

Why does it matter?

Employees represent the greatest cost and greatest opportunity in most businesses. The wage bill is by far the most significant expense for most businesses so getting the right people is important.

Plus, getting recruitment wrong can be really problematic for a business. It is now much harder to get rid of underperforming employees than it used to be. A poor employee can also disrupt a team and cause upset as others need to cover their poor performance, which can of course increase employee churn (Chapter 54). And sadly it's usually not the person you want to get rid of that leaves. Recruitment channel analytics can help to ensure you recruit the right people from the start.

Recruitment channel analytics should be conducted at least once a year so that you can use the most cost-effective channels and avoid the recruitment channels that are either not working or attracting the wrong types of candidate.

What business questions is it helping me to answer?

Recruitment channel analytics helps you answer business questions such as:

- How were your high-value employees recruited?
- Are there any patterns of trends that would indicate one channel better than another?
- Is hiring a recruitment consultant cost-effective in the long run?
- What are the most cost-effective recruitment channels for our different job positions?

How do I use it?

Recruitment analytics will involve some historical assessment of employee value using key performance indicators such as human capital value added (HCVA) and return per employee (RPE). These will help you to identify who your most productive and valuable employees are.

Surveys can also be used to gather more data (Chapters 19 and 20) which can then be mined (Chapter 6) for additional insights. You can also conduct entry interviews (Chapter 22) to establish where a candidate found the opportunity or how they came to know about the position. Correlation analysis (Chapter 3) and regression analysis (Chapter 7) can also help you to identify patterns or connections between high-value recruits and recruitment channels that you may not have been aware of.

The best results come from mixing qualitative and quantitative insights – from referral rates, to quality of candidate, quality of hire, candidate and manager satisfaction – and combine this with cost-to-hire, time-to-hire data.

The purpose of recruitment channel analytics is to predict ease of recruitment in the future and allow you to use only channels that yield high-value candidates, while hopefully minimising your need for expensive recruitment consultants.

Practical example

Hiring employees can be a costly and time-consuming process. If you use a recruitment consultant there are often significant fees. While they will find suitable candidates and screen those candidates, which will save you valuable interview time, the costs can be prohibitive, especially for senior positions.

Recruitment channel analytics can therefore help you identify that for your business online recruitment seems the most effective. Correlation analysis may identify that your high-value candidates always held positions prior to starting with you for three years or longer. These insights can then be used to fine tune the assessment process and knock out any candidate that does not meet that criterion.

That way you can stop using your recruitment firm and switch all your recruitment activity to online services.

Tips and traps

Aggregator sites like glassdoor.com operate like Trip Advisor for recruitment and can provide companies with independent reviews of their recruitment process. It is still early days for these sites, but they will become an invaluable source of information in years to come.

It is often hard to get information from candidates that didn't go for the job or didn't get a job offer, so part of your data set is incomplete – but again, sites like glassdoor.com can help with getting this kind of information as well as social media data.

Further reading and references

For more on recruitment channel analytics see for example:

- Sesil, J.C. (2013) *Applying Advanced Analytics to HR Management Decisions: Methods for Selection, Developing Incentives, and Improving Collaboration*, Upper Saddle River, NJ: Pearson FT Press
- http://www.ere.net/2008/07/07/6-good-metrics/
- http://monitor.icef.com/2013/12/big-data-predictive-modelling-and-international-student-recruitment
- http://www.glassdoor.co.uk/Reviews/index.htm

Competency
acquisition analytics

56

What is it?

Competency acquisition analytics is the process of assessing how well or otherwise your business acquires talent. Talent recruitment and management is often critically important for the growth of most businesses.

That said, the competition for talent is fierce and talented people can be very expensive to recruit and keep. Competency acquisition analytics can help to identify how successful your talent strategy is.

Why does it matter?

Competency acquisition analytics matters because talent matters. Ever since McKinsey & Co told the business community there was a 'War for Talent', business has been obsessed with talent. How to identify it, where to find it and how to keep it once you've recruited it!

And while there is little doubt that high-performing individuals are needed for growth, it is important to assess talent logically and not get too carried away with recruiting certain individuals at all cost. Talent can be hard work: individuals who are full of their own importance can, unless managed, end up being more trouble than they are worth. They can also alienate other members of the team. Getting the acquisition right matters because when done properly with the help of competency analytics you can avoid many of the downsides while accessing the upside.

When do I use it?

Competency acquisition analytics should be something you assess at least every year to see how well your business is doing at a) identifying the competencies you need and want, and b) finding those competencies cost-effectively.

It can be relatively easy to identify key players in any industry and if your business has deep pockets then those individuals can often be attracted to your business, but few businesses have deep enough pockets that will allow the money to talk when recruiting talent. Besides, individuals who only take a role because of the money will probably not stay that long or fully engage in the vision of the business. Finding ways to identify talent before it is fully fledged talent is the key, and this type of analytics allows you to do that.

It is therefore important to know how well your business is performing in the task of identifying talent early and stepping in to secure it at a reasonable price.

What business questions is it helping me to answer?

Competency acquisition analytics helps you answer business questions such as:

- Are we aware of the competencies we need? If so, what are they?
- What are the key gaps in competencies we require?
- How effective are we at attracting individuals with the right competencies to our business?

How do I use it?

A good starting point is the identification of the competencies your business requires now and in the future. You don't want to look at every little competence, just the key ones that will help you stay competitive. This can be achieved using a number of tools and techniques such as focus groups (Chapter 21), interviews (Chapter 22) and surveys (Chapters 19 and 20). It is usually relatively easy to identify the key competencies required. For more complex organisations it might make sense to apply tools such as data mining (Chapter 6) or text analytics (Chapter 8) to identify key competencies.

The next step is then to assess the current levels of these competencies within your business and the gap between what you would like to have in terms of competencies and what you actually have at present. Again, you can use similar techniques to the one listed above to perform this.

It is then a good idea to create regular assessments and updates to that model so that you can track progress over time. For example, you would want some information on whether you are able to close the competency gaps in your business and which competencies you find most difficult to acquire.

Once you have identified the key competencies required, you can monitor how effective you are at spotting and recruiting candidates with those competencies.

Practical example

As with many sports, new baseball talent was 'spotted' by experts and talent scouts who would travel the country watching baseball games in the hope they would be able to identify an upcoming star. The process was very subjective. For the most part it was down to experience and luck.

Baseball advisor Bill James changed all that. He developed a scientific evidence-based approach to 'spotting' new baseball talent that broke a player's behaviour and actions down into multiple measurable elements.

Billy Beane, the general manager of the Oakland Athletics (or the Oakland A's) heard about James's theory and decided to work with him to acquire competency or talent. Despite having the third-lowest payroll in the league, James's hypothesis worked – the Oakland A's bought undervalued talent, which in turn took the club to the playoffs in 2002 and 2003. Prior to this evidence-data-driven approach they were simply not able to successfully compete with deep-pocketed baseball clubs like the New York Yankees. Competency acquisition analytics changed all that and changed their fortune.

Tips and traps

Competency acquisition analytics is only going to be successful if you are able to effectively identify and track competencies in your organisation. Many companies don't concentrate on the vital (or difficult to get) competencies and instead produce generic competency frameworks that make the process of tracking and assessing competencies very complex and cumbersome. Key to effective competency acquisition analytics is focusing on a small set of key competencies.

Further reading and references

For more on competency acquisition analytics see for example:

- Dubois, D.D. and Rothwell, W.J. (2010) *Competency-Based Human Resource Management: Discover a New System for Unleashing the Productive Power of Exemplary Performers*, Boston, MA: Nicholas Brealey North America
- http://www.recruitingtrends.com/thought-leadership/62-how-big-data-can-turn-talent-acquisition-pros-into-superstars

Employee performance analytics

What is it?

Employee performance analytics seeks to assess individual employee performance. The resulting insights can identify who is performing well and who may need some additional training or support in order to lift their game.

Plus, an understanding of employee performance can also feed into the recruitment process so more of the right types of employees are recruited and the costly mistakes are avoided.

Why does it matter?

Employee performance analytics matters because your business needs capable high-performing employees to survive and thrive. Great companies need great people.

Unless you measure performance it can easily get lost in the day-to-day operations of the business. A poor employee can effectively be carried by a productive one, which will eventually irritate the productive employee. Your job is to know who is doing what and who needs support so that you can provide that support and lift performance across the board.

If you are seeking growth and improved profitability you need to develop and motivate your employees in order to maintain the skill level required and to ensure you keep your talented employees. Employee productivity analytics can help you do that.

When do I use it?

Most companies assess employee performance annually, this is not enough. Traditionally, line managers would conduct performance review interviews (Chapter 22) to assess an employee's performance based on some data.

In order to be effective, performance should be assessed on a regular and less formal basis and modern data collection methods allow us to collect data from many different sources to aid in the assessment.

If done well, performance analytics provide a positive experience that contributes to the overall employment and career development experience and helps to strengthen the relationship between line managers and their reports.

What business questions is it helping me to answer?

Employee performance analytics helps you answer business questions such as:

- How productive are my employees?
- Are there star performers and if so who are they?
- Are there employees who are struggling and if so who are they?
- Are there employees who are flourishing in certain tasks or who seem to outperform others in key areas?
- What are they doing differently that is making them so successful?

How do I use it?

By its nature, performance analytics is backward looking. It is assessing past performance and how an employee has performed throughout the previous year. As such it is not that useful for predicting future performance.

Today, we have many innovative ways of collecting and analysing performance, from crowd-sourced performance assessments to sensors. For example, Sociometric Solutions puts sensors into employee name badges that can detect social dynamics in the workplace. The sensors report on how employees move around the workplace, with whom they speak, and even the tone of voice they use when communicating.

One of the company's clients, a major bank, noticed that its top-performing employees at call centres were those who took breaks together. They instituted group break policies and performance improved 23 per cent.

The data collected about employee performance can, however, be further analysed to provide additional insights. They can, for example, be recorded which can then be analysed using voice analysis (Chapter 12), or converted to text for text analysis (Chapter 8), or data mining (Chapter 6). Regression analysis (Chapter 7) is also useful here to help identify any patterns that you may not have been conscious of that can then improve ongoing performance and recruitment.

Practical example

Employee performance analytics can be particularly useful in industries that traditionally have a high staff turnover such as call centres. It is important to understand the different call lengths for each operative, how many calls they get through per hour, how many of their calls escalate into issues and how many end in resolution and a happy customer.

These and countless other data points also allow you to detect patterns and identify your star performers so that what they do can be replicated by others. These insights can also be used to fine tune customer processes, recruitment and training and development initiatives so that you get more great employees and fewer poor ones. Not only does that improve results but it can significantly reduce staff turnover and recruitment costs.

Tips and traps

Whenever you monitor performance of employees it is important to be aware of the fact that the monitoring itself will affect performance. Usually when people know that specific elements of their job are monitored they make sure they perform particularly well at them. This can skew their attention away from doing a good job to simply focusing on the things that are being monitored and analysed.

With modern data capture techniques such as video and sensor data, it is possible to analyse performance more holistically with less focus on specific parts of a job that might cause the employee to skew their behaviour.

In call centres, for example, overall performance improved when companies started to record all calls and then applied analytics and random 'listen ins' to evaluate performance, rather than simply being based on call volume and call duration stats.

Further reading and references

To understand more about employee performance analytics see for example:

- Kinley, N. and Ben-Hur, S. (2013) *Talent Intelligence: What You Need to Know to Identify and Measure Talent*, 1st edition, San Francisco, CA: Jossey-Bass
- Dearborn, J. (2015) *Data Driven: How Performance Analytics Delivers Extraordinary Sales Results*, 1st edition, Hoboken, NJ: Wiley
- http://www.ehow.com/about_6469908_employee-performance-analysis.html
- http://www.cioinsight.com/it-management/workplace/slideshows/improving-employee-performance-with-data-analysis-02
- http://smallbusiness.chron.com/conduct-statistical-analysis-job-performance-47731.html
- https://www.linkedin.com/pulse/20140701052815–64875646-beware-big-data-in-your-workplace
- https://hbr.org/2012/06/crowdsource-your-performance-r

Corporate culture analytics

58

Culture is notoriously difficult to pinpoint and even harder to change. It is essentially the collective often unspoken rules, systems and patterns of behaviour that embody your business. Culture is not something that can be hung on the wall like a values statement – it shows up as the collective actions of the people in the business.

The challenge with culture is that what people think it is and what business owners might like it to be is often considerably different from what it actually is in the business. Corporate culture analytics is therefore the process of assessing and understanding more about your corporate culture or the different cultures that exist across your organisation. This then allows you to track changes in culture you would like to make, understand how the culture is changing, create early warning systems to detect toxic cultures in their development and ensure you are recruiting people that don't clash with the corporate culture.

Why does it matter?

Corporate culture analytics matters because it can provide valuable information and insights that can allow you to uncover the genuine culture of the business, and those insights can be used to amplify the good bits and help change the unhelpful parts.

Part of the reason culture is so difficult to change is that the people in the business don't fully appreciate what it is to start with. This type of analytics can lift the lid on culture which can in turn influence strategy.

When do I use it?

Corporate culture is usually fairly stable. Once you have assessed it, you can then put systems in place to track key elements of that culture in a more ongoing fashion where you use snapshot data collections to create early warning systems of a mismatch between the culture you would like to have and what the data is showing you.

What business questions is it helping me to answer?

Corporate culture analytics helps you answer business questions such as:

- What is the corporate culture?
- How is our corporate culture changing?
- Are the behaviours of our employees in line with the culture we want?

How do I use it?

The most obvious tools for culture analytics are to use surveys (Chapters 19 and 20), focus group research (Chapter 21) or employee interviews (Chapter 22).

The challenge with those approaches is that people can tell you what they think you want to hear. Plus they can be expensive.

There are now many more analytic tools that can be used to give a better and more accurate insight into corporate culture. You can, for example, collect data from internal intranet sites, social media and internal written communication.

This data can then be analysed using text analytics (Chapter 8) and sentiment analysis (Chapter 9).

You can also use neural network analysis to assess the internal networks within the business and who is connected to who (Chapter 17) as well as ethnography (Chapter 23) to get in-depth insights into the company culture. This can be particularly useful if you are seeking to change the culture because it will highlight who the influencers are in your business. If you want to effect change you need to get those people on board.

Practical example

You may believe that your corporate culture is efficient but fun. You may think that your business operates like a family with strong focus on value for money and strong customer service. Over the years you may even have sought to drive that message home to your employees.

Your orientation for new recruits draws new employees' attention to those values and the corporate culture that you believe exists. But what happens after six months – are those employees the living expression of those values or is something else calling the shots?

You could ask your new employee or you could conduct annual surveys but the quickest way to get to the truth is to assess what your employees are saying and doing as part of their day-to-day life. That's your culture. If you believe you are driven by high-quality customer service and yet no one answers the phone after 4.45 p.m. then chances are it's not quite so real in your business as you would like it to be.

Corporate culture analytics can shine a light into your business so you can determine if your culture is positive and helpful, or in need of an overhaul.

Tips and traps

If you record customer service conversations these voice recordings can provide a rich vein of data to assess corporate culture. You can apply voice analytics (Chapter 12) to this data or convert to text and use text analytics tools (Chapter 8).

Culture assessments are also a great opportunity for qualitative and immersive analysis techniques such as ethnography (Chapter 23). Be sure to approach this analytic progress from a quantitative and qualitative perspective otherwise you can get a skewed picture.

Further reading and references

For more on corporate culture analytics see for example:

- Sartain, L. and Daily, B. (2013) *Cracking the Culture Code*, 1st edition, Boulder, CO: RoundPegg
- Rosaldo, R. (1993) *Culture & Truth: The Remaking of Social Analysis*, Boston, MA: Beacon Press
- http://www.ehow.com/about_5270081_corporate-culture-analysis.html
- http://web.mit.edu/anthropology/pdf/articles/fischer/fischer_cultural_analysis.pdf
- http://feaa.ucv.ro/annals/v1_2012/EVMM-11.pdf

59

Leadership analytics

What is it?

Leadership analytics seeks to uncover how good leadership is in your business. So much of leadership is subjective. We are told that great leaders are born not made, but is that really true? Leadership analytics unpacks the various dimensions of leadership performance via data to uncover the good, the bad and the ugly.

Why does it matter?

Leadership analytics matters because leadership matters. Poor leadership, whether of a business, division or team costs money and prevents a business from fulfilling its potential.

If a leader is poor at empowering and engaging his or her employees then this will impact results, productivity and profit.

When do I use it?

Leadership is best assessed on an ongoing basis, if that is not possible then you can assess it in regular intervals – for example, every six months or so.

However, if someone is new to a leadership role then it is probably wise to perform leadership analytics more frequently to track their early progress. This will allow you to pick up any failings early so as to get the individual back on track.

What business questions is it helping me to answer?

Leadership analytics helps you answer business questions such as:

- How good are the leaders in the business?
- What do our employees think and feel about their leader?

- What leadership style is most appropriate in our business?
- Does anyone in the business who is currently not a leader demonstrate leadership potential?

How do I use it?

Data about the leadership performance can be gained through the use of surveys (Chapters 19 and 20), focus groups (Chapter 21), employee interviews (Chapter 22) or ethnography (Chapter 23). It is advisable to make the data collection anonymous for the employees to open up and really provide useful information. Few employees would feel confident or safe talking about their leader or manager if they knew that person could or may have access to their opinion.

It is also possible to conduct behaviour profiling of leaders. Really good leaders tend to demonstrate certain personality traits or characteristics. These can be generic attributes or you can analyse your existing leadership cadre to identify what the really good ones have that the less successful ones don't. These insights can be used to direct training and support programmes as well as the recruitment process.

Text analytics (Chapter 8) is a very powerful way of extracting key leadership characteristics, both of good and not so good leaders.

You can then use correlation analysis (Chapter 3) and regression analysis (Chapter 7) to compare good leadership with actual performance results, which you can assess using financial metrics as well as data such as employee satisfaction or churn.

Practical example

In an effort to raise leadership performance in their management Google set out to answer two questions:

1 'What is it that makes a great manager?'
2 'What are the behaviours that make managers struggle?'

Based on some extensive leadership performance analytics including interviews with their managers, 360-degree feedback surveys of their employees, and regression analysis of things such as job performance and employee satisfaction, Google was able to identify eight behaviours that make a great manager in Google:

1 Is a good coach.
2 Empowers the team and does not micromanage.
3 Expresses interest/concern for team members' success and personal wellbeing.
4 Is productive and results-orientated.
5 Is a good communicator – listens and shares information.
6 Helps with career development.

7 Has a clear vision/strategy for the team.

8 Has important technical skills that help him/her advise the team.

In addition, the research alerted them to the top three reasons why managers were struggling in their role:

1 Has a tough transition (e.g. suddenly promoted, hired from outside with little training).

2 Lacks a consistent philosophy/approach to performance management and career development.

3 Spends too little time on managing and communicating.

Acting on these valuable insights Google now gear the 360-degree feedback surveys for managers around these aspects and it is conducted twice a year. This therefore instigates an early warning system to detect both great and struggling managers. Plus, Google has revised its management training and recruitment in light of their findings.

Tips and traps

While there are some generic leadership assessment models that you could use in your business, it is always better to create your own model based on what leadership characteristics you value in your particular corporate culture.

Draw on data and insights from other analytics tools such as employee performance analytics (Chapter 57) and corporate culture analytics (Chapter 58) to help you establish what is going to make a great leader in *your* business.

This was why Google were so successful in their quest to identify leadership excellence – they took the time to figure out what leadership excellence looked like in their unique culture.

Further reading and references

For further insight into leadership analytics see for example:

- Wall, T. and Knights, J. (2013) *Leadership Assessment for Talent Development*, London: Kogan Page
- http://ezinearticles.com/?Leadership-Analytics&id=2255024
- http://www.jqassociates.com/assessment/tools/leadership-effectiveness-analysis.asp

[PART SEVEN]

Operational analytics

Fraud detection
analytics

60

What is it?

Fraud detection analytics is the process of uncovering fraudulent actions or behaviour so that you can then predict fraud and reduce or stop it.

This type of analytics looks at vast amounts of data to identify patterns or certain behaviours that flag fraudulent activity so that processes or systems can be changed to prevent fraudulent activity.

Why does it matter?

Fraud detection analytics matters because it can help you to identify patterns of behaviour or actions that are the precursors to customer or employee fraud, and therefore stop it before it happens.

Fraud costs many businesses a great deal of money every year – money that could be bolstering profits and allowing the business to grow. And it can happen in every company from the fraudulent use of an expense account to customers making fraudulent insurance claims to credit card fraud by organised criminal groups. Online fraud is also a growing area and every business needs to be vigilant – small or large. In fact, often small companies are particularly vulnerable because they assume that the criminals will be targeting larger businesses. This is a mistake because often smaller businesses are easier targets for criminals who can, for example, remotely access your network or manufacturing systems and demand a ransom before giving you back control. Clearly analysing your vulnerabilities is incredibly important so you can stay one step ahead.

When do I use it?

How often you conduct fraud detection analytics will depend on the nature of your business. Credit card companies and insurance firms are assessing for fraud on a constant basis. If an individual makes a purchase on their credit card that is unusual, for example, then they will usually get a phone call from their credit card company almost immediately. This is because algorithms have assessed your normal credit card activity and geographic location and anything outside those and many other parameters raise a red flag. For example, if your credit card is used in London at 11 a.m. and then used in Glasgow at 12 noon this is clearly fraudulent activity because it's not possible to get to Glasgow from London in one hour.

Even if you don't operate in high-risk fraud areas such as finance or insurance you should conduct fraud detection analytics at least every six months.

What business questions is it helping me to answer?

Fraud detection analytics helps you answer business questions such as:

- Are any of our customers engaged in fraudulent activity against your business?
- Are any employees engaged in fraudulent activity against your business?
- Are there any warning signs or patterns that indicate fraud is imminent so that we can intervene and stop it before it happens?

How do I use it?

Activity, written and spoken data offer a rich vein of information from which to conduct fraud detection analytics. You can, for example, use CCTV footage to monitor warehouses and picking and packing areas. Video analytics (Chapter 11) can be applied to this data to extract insights, while voice recordings can also be used for analysis (Chapter 12).

For example, customer service calls are usually recorded; voice analytics can identify stress levels in a customer's voice which may sometimes indicate fraud. This type of analysis could be especially helpful on insurance claim helplines. When someone is scared, stressed or lying, they exhibit vocal clues that can be picked up by voice analytics. Of course the person may be stressed because they've just had their home burgled, but this type of technique can at least flag those cases that need a closer look to root out those that are lying and minimise insurance fraud.

Text on forms, emails or social media can also be used for text analytics (Chapter 8). And data mining (Chapter 6) and correlation analysis (Chapter 3) can be used to identify patterns of behaviour or connections between seemingly random activities that could indicate fraud.

Practical example

Insurance companies use data mining and factor analysis on their online application forms and were able to find a correlation between the time a customer took to fill in their online claim form and fraud. This can be indicated by either filling the form in too slowly or too quickly. Often when a customer takes too long to complete the form, or hovers over a field for too long, they are thinking too hard about what happened or what they should write. This can indicate they are not being entirely truthful about the event.

Of course this is not the only assessment – the insurance companies allow for the fact that sometimes the person may just be slow. Perhaps they were interrupted by someone at the door, or they need to take their children to ballet class or they are older and not very good with computers. But this data will raise a red flag that is collated with other data points such as how many times a person changed the data in a particular field. If too many red flags are raised then the insurance assessor knows to look more closely at the case.

Conversely if the form is completed too quickly this can also raise alarm bells. Criminals often use bots (i.e. an automated web robot) to complete forms, or they will cut and paste from previous claim forms making the completion process very quick.

The same insurance company also monitors how we fill in application forms online. This can show them how often we retype data into certain boxes to attempt to get a better quote when we say our car is parked in a garage rather than on the road. Big data analytics tools are now watching out for this type of behaviour and will flag any potential fraud.

Tips and traps

Fraud detection is a constantly evolving area because the ways people perpetuate fraud is constantly evolving. Don't decide on patterns or red flags and simply then test for them – you need to run full-scale analysis fairly frequently to identify how fraud is changing. Also, ask your employees and customer services people to be on the lookout for new and novel ways that customers are finding to defraud the business.

Once you find fraudulent activity, also run some data mining on those cases to see if you can identify patterns that you can then use to prevent future fraud. For example, if there any demographics data that would indicate a 'type' of customer to steer clear of?

Further reading and references

For more on fraud detection analytics see for example:

- Spann, D.D. (2013) *Fraud Analytics: Strategies and Methods for Detection and Prevention*, 1st edition, Hoboken, NJ: Wiley

- Gee, S. (2014) *Fraud and Fraud Detection, + Website: A Data Analytics Approach*, 1st edition, Hoboken, NJ: Wiley
- Baesens, B. and Van Vlasselaer, V. (2015) *Fraud Analytics Using Descriptive, Predictive, and Social Network Techniques: a Guide to Data Science for Fraud Detection*, 1st edition, Hoboken, NJ: Wiley
- http://www.sap.com/pc/analytics/governance-risk-compliance/software/fraud-management/index.html
- http://www.acl.com/pdfs/DP_Fraud_detection_BANKING.pdf
- http://www.infosys.com/FINsights/Documents/pdf/issue10/insurance-fraud-detection.pdf

Core competency analytics

61

What is it?

Core competency analytics is the process of identifying what your core competencies are so that you may exploit them to the full.

A core competency is a management concept introduced by C.K. Prahalad and Gary Hamel, who defined the theory as 'a harmonious combination of multiple resources and skills that distinguish a firm in the marketplace'. In order to be considered core competencies they must fulfil three criteria:

1 Provide potential access to a wide variety of markets.
2 Should make a significant contribution to the perceived customer benefits of the end product.
3 Difficult to imitate by competitors.

Why does it matter?

Core competency analytics matters because finding and securing a competitive advantage is tough. It is even tougher if you are not 100 per cent sure exactly what unique core abilities your business has.

Often in business we tend to look at the end product or service we produce and consider that is what makes us unique, but core competency analytics looks behind those end products and services into how they are created, breaking the production down so that you can highlight key skills or abilities that could be utilised elsewhere for maximum advantage.

When do I use it?

Every business should know what their core competencies are so that they can optimise them; so this is a process that should be done at least every year.

Plus, if you don't know what they are and who in your business has these core competencies you may not realise that you are losing them when people move on – until it's too late.

What business questions is it helping me to answer?

Core competency analytics helps you answer business questions such as:

- What do we do better than most other businesses in our area?
- What core competencies have we accumulated over the years?
- What should be our core competencies?
- Could those core competencies be better utilised?
- Could they be successfully used to create new or different types of products?
- How developed are our core competencies?
- Where have we got gaps in our core competencies?

How do I use it?

Start by listing all the actions that are required to produce your products or services. In essence this means detailing exactly how a product is made or how a service is developed from the very start of the process to the delivery of that product or service. Taking each step or element in turn, break it down to understand what enables competency in that task or process so you have a map of how something is achieved.

You can then start identifying patterns (using, for example, factor analysis) to determine what are the core competencies in your business.

Practical example

A large car manufacturer may believe that their core competency is in manufacturing cars, but by running core competency analytics they learn that this isn't the case. Instead, by breaking the manufacturing process down and analysing each area they soon discover that their core competency is actually the design and manufacture of engines.

This insight therefore allows them to explore new market opportunities where brilliant engine design could be a major competitive advantage beyond the creation of cars. As a result, the traditional car manufacturer can move into the creation of lawnmowers, tractors or any other areas where engine design is important.

This makes sense in business. If you have the core ability and skill set that already puts you ahead of your competition then why wouldn't you then further utilise that same skill set to expand into new markets.

Tips and traps

Identifying core competencies can help to identify and eliminate waste or improve inefficiencies as a by-product of the identification process. It can also help to identify areas of development before they arise to cause significant problems.

For example, if the car manufacturer in the example didn't appreciate that their core competency was engine design then if their most experienced engineer announced he was retiring or resigning to pursue other opportunities they may not see that as the challenge that it really is.

Further reading and references

For more on core competency analytics see for example:

- http://www.mindtools.com/pages/article/newTMC_94.htm
- http://www.ehow.com/about_5426468_competencies-analysis.html
- http://www.demandmetric.com/content/core-competencies-assessment
- http://www.thwink.org/soft/info/process/CoreCompetence.html
- http://www.tutor2u.net/business/strategy/core_competencies.htm

62

Supply chain analytics

What is it?

Supply chain analytics is the process of assessing each stage of your supply chain or the various processes that go into creating your product or service. This type of analysis looks at all the processes from purchasing the raw materials, through various production processes to final delivery to the customer so as to manage inventory intelligently, deliver to your customer efficiently and minimise costs and delays.

The purpose of supply chain analytics is to determine opportunities for savings, improvements or increased return, while also ensuring that your customers get what they ordered as quickly as possible.

Why does it matter?

Supply chain analytics matters because you need to know what happens in your business between the moment you purchase from your suppliers to the moment your customers receive their goods so that you can control costs, price your products or services correctly, make money and keep your customers happy.

The more you understand your supply chain and the more flexible it is the better able you will be to understand your market, predict potential road bumps that could cause your business problems and the quicker you can adapt to changing customer needs. Plus, by understanding your supply chain you can effectively predict how many products or services you will need to supply demand, which can in turn allow you to minimise inventory and the costly need for excessive warehousing.

When do I use it?

Although supply chain analytics may still be relevant if you are providing a service, it is more important when you produce and sell products. In which case you should be conducting supply chain analytics at least every month.

If there are few changes in your supply chain and the business is fairly stable then you may get away with every six months.

What business questions is it helping me to answer?

Supply chain analytics helps you answer business questions such as:

- What is the optimal delivery route for our trucks?
- Where are the delays occurring in the supply chain?
- Are there any significant fluctuations in supply performance?
- Which suppliers are more unpredictable and why?

How do I use it?

With sensors and data collections along most supply chains, it can be easy to track actual performance. The data can come from telematics systems on delivery trucks, from GPS tracking sensors on ships and lorries, as well as from RFID (radio frequency identification) sensors on pallets and products and cameras.

This allows companies to track products from the manufacturing process right through to the end user. This data can then be correlated with other supply chain metrics: such as order fulfilment cycle time (OFCT), which is the continuous measurement defined as the time from order confirmation to receipt of the goods or services; or delivery in full on time (DIFOT), which looks specifically at the fulfilment process which is all the customer is really interested in anyway.

Analysing this data using tools including neural network analysis (Chapter 17), linear programming (Chapter 14) and Monte Carlo simulation (Chapter 13) can allow you to optimise delivery routes and detect bottlenecks and risks in your supply chain.

Practical example

I worked with a major drinks manufacturer that was interested in discovering their shrinkage rates across their supply chain from production through distribution to the retailers. In other words, they wanted to see where they lost most product, either though breakages or theft. The idea was obviously to identify problem areas and then institute processes or better packaging that would prevent this costly expense. The result of the supply chain analytics using tracking sensors (Chapter 26), image analysis (Chapter 10), interviews (Chapter 22) as well as elements of ethnography (Chapter 23) showed that their supply chain was very secure and the vast majority of their shrinkage resulted in the retail setting where people were stealing the product from supermarkets. By working with the supermarkets to ensure better tagging they were able to reduce shrinkage considerably.

Many manufacturers are also now using sensors on their manufacturing equipment that monitor real-time operation of the equipment. These sensors will provide data on wear and tear so that parts of important machinery can be replaced at the right time – before they break down and cause disruption to production. This enables dynamic servicing, which is more effective and often much cheaper than replacing parts simply because a certain amount of time has elapsed.

Sensors can also raise issues that may not be noticeable from operators and also provide important data on usage and productivity.

In days gone by, if you bought a product you might get a delivery window of several hours. Those days are now gone because of sensors on pallets and the use of handheld devices that record delivery to monitor where drivers are, while also monitoring the engines of the delivery vehicles to create dynamic servicing, etc. It is now possible also to track your order online. Not only do you know when your product will be delivered – often to within an hour window or less – but you might even know the delivery driver's name!

Tips and traps

Amazon is a global leader in supply chain management – there isn't much they haven't figured out. Amazon has obviously developed software to optimise their stock, but it isn't possible to purchase this software so you must use these analytics tools for your own business.

Making money in business is not just about making sales – it is also about managing costs and supply chain analytics offers a powerful insight into where and how you can manage costs effectively.

Supply chain analytics makes sense – using big data, predictive tools and cloud computing to crunch through vast amounts of data to optimise the supply chain makes business sense. But often the supply chain systems are not cut out to deliver the type of data that is required to crunch. The biggest trap therefore is often the investment required to make use of the main tools now available.

Further reading and references

To understand more about supply chain analytics see for example:

- Sanders, N.R. (2014) *Big Data Driven Supply Chain Management: A Framework for Implementing Analytics and Turning Information Into Intelligence*, Upper Saddle River, NJ: Pearson FT Press
- Plenert, G.J. (2014) *Supply Chain Optimisation through Segmentation and Analytics,* 1st edition, Hove: CRC Press
- http://www.sas.com/resources/asset/SAS_IW_FinalLoRes.pdf
- http://www.industryweek.com/blog/supply-chain-analytics-what-it-and-why-it-so-important

- http://www.ebnonline.com/author.asp?id=1061&doc_id=262988&itc=velocity_ticker
- http://www.information-age.com/technology/information-management/123456972/tesco-saves-millions-with-supply-chain-analytics
- http://sloanreview.mit.edu/article/are-predictive-analytics-transforming-your-supply-chain/
- http://papers.ssrn.com/sol3/papers.cfm?abstract_id=2279482

63

Lean Six Sigma analytics

What is it?

Lean Six Sigma analytics is the process of analysing efficiency and quality in your business. Traditionally used in manufacturing, Lean Six Sigma is now also being used in service industries such as insurance companies where the claim handling process is constantly being improved.

The lean part of the equation looks at seven different types of waste to identify areas for improvement:

1 **Transportation:** Is there any unnecessary transportation or handling of goods that is adding cost or wasting time?

2 **Motion:** Is there any unnecessary motion of people or equipment? In other words, are there any people or equipment that is being moved too often or being moved about too frequently?

3 **Inventory:** Is there any work-in-progress (WIP), or finished goods that are in excess of requirements or don't have a value-adding function?

4 **Waiting:** Is there any waste caused when people, parts, systems or facilities sit idle, waiting for a work cycle to be completed?

5 **Over-production:** Is there any waste caused by producing more or faster quantities than the customer is demanding? For example, if production is making larger batch sizes than is ordered.

6 **Over-processing:** Is there any unnecessary work that goes beyond what is required to satisfy customer requirements?

7 **Defects:** Is there any waste caused by anything that the customer would deem unacceptable.

Lean Six Sigma analytics provides data on the level of waste in your internal processes that will in turn allow you to become more efficient and profitable.

The Six Sigma part is more about quality and the elimination of defects. The term 'Six Sigma' comes from the field of statistics and evaluates process capability.

Technically speaking, 'Six Sigma' means that your defect level is below 3.4 per million opportunities. In other words, for every million actions or steps in a production process an error is made less than 3.4 times! That said, each business that uses Six Sigma needs to determine their own appropriate sigma level.

What makes Six Sigma so useful is that it is a measurement tool focused on verifiable data and statistical methods, rather than assumptions and guesswork, *and* it is a performance improvement methodology.

Why does it matter?

Lean Six Sigma analytics matters because efficiency and quality matter in any business and this type of analysis seeks to establish how efficiently you operate and whether your products or services are of a consistently high quality.

This is clearly important because your customers are buying from you expecting a certain quality and you need to know a) what that is, and b) whether you are meeting their expectations or not. Operational efficiency is also critical in a successful business because it provides an opportunity to cut unnecessary cost and therefore make more money.

When do I use it?

You should know what sort of quality you are producing and the efficiency of your processes at all times. As a result you should be using Six Sigma analytics more or less constantly.

What business questions is it helping me to answer?

Lean Six Sigma analytics helps you answer business questions such as:

- What is the quality of the product or service we produce?
- Has this improved, remained constant or dropped over the last few months?
- If there have been changes to the quality, what has caused these changes?
- Are there any areas of our business that could be made more efficient?
- Are there opportunities to save money that we are currently not exploiting?

How do I use it?

The Six Sigma process (which was pioneered by Motorola in the late 1980s and later adopted very successfully by global giants such as General Electric and Honeywell, as well as many other companies of various sizes), informs managers as to the stability and predictability of process results. The goal is that process defect or error rates will be no more 3.4 per one million opportunities.

As an analogy, consider a goalkeeper of a football team who plays 50 games in a season and who in each game faces 50 shots from the opposing team. If a defect is when the team scores, then a Six Sigma goalkeeper would concede one goal every 147 years!

It is important to stress that Six Sigma is both a measure and a performance improvement methodology. As a methodology Six Sigma represents a set of tools that enable continuous or preferably breakthrough performance. These tools are based on the DMAIC principles:

- **D**efine customer requirements (internal or external); that is their expectation of the process.
- **M**easure the current performance; what is the frequency of defects?
- **A**nalyse the data collected and map to determine cause and effect and opportunities for improvement; why, when and where the defects occur?
- **I**mprove the target process by designing solutions to improve, fix or prevent problems.
- **C**ontrol the improvements to keep the process on the new course; how can we ensure that the process stays fixed?

DMAIC implementation is through an in-house team of Six Sigma-certified employees, known as Master Black Belts, Black Belts or Green Belts depending on their experience and levels of involvement.

In essence, the promise is that by reaching Six Sigma performance levels, customer dissatisfaction will decrease significantly and that, ultimately, superior and sustainable financial results will be achieved.

Practical example

As a clothing manufacturer you may have a number or retail customers who buy your product to sell in their shops. Each order, however, may be slightly different, not just in the styles and numbers of garments bought but also the tolerance that each supplier will accept.

For example, you may supply jeans to a large supermarket chain which they then sell as part of their own-label clothing range. The supermarket's order may include 1,000 pairs of jeans in various sizes. If the supermarket has asked for 400 pairs of size-30 jeans, 400 pairs of size-32 jeans and 200 pairs of size-34 jeans they will not accept the order if anything else is delivered. This can be very costly for you. Lean Six Sigma analytics ensures that the required tolerances are adhered to and minimum defects. The supermarket may accept all size-32 jeans with a waist size of 31.8–32.2 inches, i.e. a 0.2-inch tolerance.

Most customers realise that each pair of jeans that is manufactured is not 100 per cent identical. However, if another of your clients was a high-end fashion retailer who was going to put a high-value brand name on the jeans then they may only accept the order if there is a 0.1-inch tolerance or less. Lean Six Sigma analytics allows you to manage this process.

Tips and traps

A common criticism of Six Sigma is that the projects are typically implemented bottom-up. As a result, organisations spend a lot of efforts on projects that look at tiny areas of their business. This way they pick the lowest-hanging fruits but often miss the big opportunities. The biggest benefits from Six Sigma are secured when projects are related to the achievement of strategic goals. Six Sigma teams should choose strategically relevant projects and not just those that delver some financial gains.

Linked to the above, it is telling to note that although some of the organisations that became poster boys for Six Sigma have indeed secured mouthwatering cost savings from their efforts, they have simultaneously been very poor performers on the stock market and have been recognised for their strategic failures. The argument has been that these organisations have been exclusively focused on using Six Sigma to identify cost-saving opportunities rather than as a tool to continuously improve performance against a strategic goal: this is not how to get the best from Six Sigma projects.

Further reading and references

For more on Lean Six Sigma analytics see for example:

- Pande, P.S., Neuman, R.P. and Cavanagh, R.R. (2000) *The Six Sigma Way: How GE, Motorola, and Other Top Companies are Honing Their Performance*, New York: McGraw-Hill

- www.sixsigmaonline.org

- www.6sigma.us

- http://www.tutorialspoint.com/six_sigma/six_sigma_measure_phase.htm

- http://www.ehow.com/about_7296799_difference-six-sigma-six-sigma.html

- http://www.processexcellencenetwork.com/lean-six-sigma-business-transformation/articles/case-study-using-six-sigma-to-reduce-excess-invent

- http://www.qualitydigest.com/inside/quality-insider-column/three-types-lean-six-sigma-projects.html

- http://www.miconleansixsigma.com/six-sigma-tutorial.html

64 Capacity utilisation analytics

What is it?

Capacity utilisation analytics is similar to capacity analytics (Chapter 53), but instead the focus here is on equipment and plant rather than people.

Why does it matter?

Capacity utilisation analytics matters because it affects efficiency, productivity and ultimately profit.

If you have invested in expensive machinery or equipment then you need to know how often that equipment is being used in relation to how often it could be used. If you realise that critical machinery is sitting idle then you can't manage that capacity more appropriately to increase productivity and therefore potentially increase revenue.

When do I use it?

Most modern equipment is full of inbuilt sensors that can effectively measure capacity utilisation on a constant basis. These sensors will provide a wealth of data, not only on how often the equipment or machinery is being used but also on how long it's being used for and how efficiently as well as how often it will need servicing to maintain optimum output.

That way you can ensure that you get the most back from your investment and minimise downtime through faults.

What business questions is it helping me to answer?

Capacity utilisation analytics helps you answer business questions such as:

- Are we getting the most out of our expensive equipment?

- How efficiently is that equipment being used?
- Where are key bottlenecks in our operational performance?

How do I use it?

Most modern machines have inbuilt sensors that collect information about their use. Modern cars collect data on how often we use them and how we are driving, which car manufacturers can use to dynamically adjust our service intervals. If we run cars or other vehicles in our business we can do the same.

We can use data from our machines to understand what percentage of the available time they are in use. This gives business an idea of their return on their investment as well as an insight into the level of spare capacity in the business. It can be used to understand to what level production could be ramped up before new capital investment in new machines would be necessary.

Companies can simply extract the data from the machines or, if they are not fitted with internal sensors, they can put sensors in place or use, for example, video analytics (Chapter 11) to determine utilisation levels.

Practical example

A hospital may use capacity utilisation analytics to measure the capacity of their equipment. For example, an MRI scanner is extremely expensive to buy, install and run. Once that investment has been made, it is important that the equipment is utilised effectively and is not sitting idle for large periods of time.

Capacity analytics would therefore look at how often the MRI scanner is used each week and how much spare capacity there is in an average week. That data could then allow the hospital to identify capacity gaps which can then be filled to increase efficiency or profit. For example, if the MRI scanner is standing unused on certain days, they could offer the equipment for hire to other hospitals or medical professionals on those days.

Tips and traps

As with so many other analytics processes, it is important not to get too carried away with analysing everything you can – concentrate on the key assets in your business.

Further reading and references

For more on capacity utilisation analytics see for example:

- http://www.fao.org/docrep/006/y5027e/y5027e06.htm

65

Project and programme analytics

Project and programme analytics is the process of assessing how effective your internal projects and programmes have been so you can improve them in the future.

There are always three key components that successful delivery is measured against:

- **Schedule** – Is the project on schedule?
- **Budget** – Is the project on budget?
- **Deliverables** – Is the project delivering the specified outcomes?

Project and programme analytics assesses performance against schedule, budget and quality of output.

Why does it matter?

Project and programme analytics matters because most strategic and change initiatives are delivered via projects or programmes. If they are unsuccessful, too disruptive or do not get finished on time, on budget or to the right standard then the implications can be felt right across the business.

Keeping an eye on project and programme performance as they progress is far better than setting out the target and crossing your fingers that it will be met. Ongoing assessment can help you to anticipate any potential problems and take evasive action to avoid challenges before they occur, or to get the project or programme back on course if it starts to slide.

When do I use it?

You should conduct project and programme analytics whenever you are implementing a new project or programme.

Knowing that they are going to be thoroughly assessed from start to finish will also help ensure that you and your management team are fully engaged in the process and are very sure that the project is required.

What business questions is it helping me to answer?

Project and programme analytics helps you answer business questions such as:

- To what extent are our projects or programmes delivered on schedule?
- To what extent are our projects or programmes delivered within budget?
- To what extent are our projects or programmes making the desired or expected progress?

How do I use it?

There are a number of key performance indicators that can help you to keep track of the various parameters that must be measured including project schedule variance, project cost variance and earned value.

In addition, projects and programmes are often launched with closed social media groups or intranets where those involved can share their experiences, ask questions and share concerns. These then offer a significant source of text data that could be analysed (Chapter 8) to spot patterns, or sentiment analysis (Chapter 9) to gauge whether the mood around the project or programme is positive, negative or neutral.

Practical example

Implementing a project or process without any follow-up assessment is a recipe for disaster and you will almost certainly run into difficulties. There are many ways for projects to fail and plenty of famous examples that demonstrate the reality when proper project and programme analytics are not conducted.

For example, the new Wembley stadium in London was originally scheduled to open in 2003 but it didn't open until 2007. The iconic Sydney Opera House was scheduled to open in 1963 at a cost of AU$7 million but actually opened in 1973 at a cost of AU$102 million. Concorde supersonic aeroplane cost 12 times more than scheduled, the Channel Tunnel between the UK and France cost 80 per cent more than budgeted for, and Boston's 'Big Dig' tunnel construction project went 275 per cent or US$11 billion over budget.

Tips and traps

Before you embark on any new project or programme make sure you are very clear about why you are investing in the process and what you expect it to deliver. It can be very easy to initiate a project because 'it's worth a try' or because 'it couldn't hurt', but the waste in resources and time can be significant so be sure you really need to analyse your project or programme before you start.

The biggest trap is that people don't fully engage with the process until they are knee deep in the project or programme and things start to go wrong.

Further reading and references

For more on project and programme analytics see for example:

- http://www.pmi.org/~/media/PDF/Knowledge-Shelf/Gera_2011%20(2).ashx
- http://www.projecttimes.com/articles/the-role-of-analytics-in-projects.html

Environmental impact analytics

66

What is it?

Environmental impact analytics is the process of assessing the impact your business has on the environment. From where you source your raw materials to your production process and delivery, environmental impact analytics are essential so that you know what is happening right along your supply chain.

This type of analytics is going to become increasingly important as legislation is brought in to combat climate change and minimise our environmental damage.

Why does it matter?

Environmental impact analytics matter because more and more customers want to know this data. They want to know where they are buying their products and services from and that those companies have acted responsibly towards the planet.

Sooner or later, business will be forced to comply through legislation and be made accountable for their impact on the environment. It is far better to know your current impact and implement improvements now before you are made to change via legislation. Right now, companies that embrace their environmental responsibilities and actively seek to minimise their negative impact can gain a competitive advantage. Once governments push through legislation, that competitive advantage will not exist because everyone will have to get on board or be penalised.

When do I use it?

Environmental impact analytics should be done annually. The initial analysis will always be the most rigorous and time-consuming, but once it has been analysed completely once, keeping tabs on your environmental impact will be much easier and quicker.

You should also use this type of analysis whenever you are looking to change parts of your supply chain or your production process to make sure that the changes will not adversely impact the environment.

What business questions is it helping me to answer?

Environmental impact analytics helps you answer business questions such as:

- What is our carbon footprint?
- What is our water footprint?
- What is our energy consumption?
- How environmentally responsible are we?
- How environmentally responsible are our suppliers?
- Are we doing more than our competitors and, if so, can we promote our environmental focus to gain a competitive advantage?

How do I use it?

There are a number of key performance indicators (KPIs) that you can use to measure your historical environmental impact. These include your carbon footprint, water footprint, energy consumption, supply chain miles, waste and product recycling rate.

Environmental impact analytics can be extremely complex and it's certainly an area that is going to be increasingly important in the future. Being able to measure and demonstrate environmental credentials can still offer a competitive advantage but the day is coming where legislation will demand it.

If this is not something you do at all right now then consider using some of the KPIs above or using specialist tools such as carbon analytics. Carbon analytics, for example, is pretty easy to apply because the approach uses information your company already has such as purchase records, supply chain data and basics like your annual turnover and industry statistics. This can then give you a 'big picture' measurement of your environmental impact. Plus, over time this tool will tailor its analysis to your company's unique profile.

Practical example

As a manufacturer you may be concerned about the resources you use in your production process. There are a variety of different 'footprints' that you can analyse to assess your impact. Ideally these assessments will give you an opportunity to reduce your footprint and use the insights to publicise your environmental efforts and credentials for better PR and potentially improved sales.

There are a variety of different 'footprints' to explore:

- **Ecological footprint** – measures how much land/ocean is required to make a certain product or provide a certain service while also measuring the damage to that land or ocean in creating that end product.

- **Materials footprint** – measures the total materials used and waste generated in creating your product or service.

- **Carbon footprint** – measures the direct and indirect greenhouse gas emissions caused by the creation of your product or service. This is one of the most developed footprint tools.

- **Nitrogen footprint** – measures the reactive nitrogen created in the production of your product or service.

- **Water footprint** – measures how much freshwater is directly or indirectly used in the production of your product or service.

Tips and traps

Taking action now when you can determine your timeline and implement incremental changes to the way you do business to ensure you are more environmentally responsible is always going to be preferable to waiting until you are forced to take action. Environmental impact analytics can help you to predict your future so you can make manageable incremental shifts.

Don't assume the world will stay the same forever – always look for ways to improve your production process to reduce waste and minimise energy and water use. Not only will this be better for the environment, it will also be better for your bottom line.

Further reading and references

For more on environmental impact analytics see for example:

- http://www.lic.wisc.edu/shapingdane/facilitation/all_resources/impacts/analysis_environmental.htm
- http://enviroliteracy.org/article.php/1286.html
- http://www.epa.gov/sustainability/analytics/life-cycle.htm
- http://www.co2analytics.com/how-it-works
- http://www.epa.gov/sustainability/analytics/environmental-footprint.htm

67

Corporate social responsibility (CSR) analytics

What is it?

Corporate social responsibility analytics is the process of assessing just how real or otherwise your stated corporate social responsibility is to reality. The spirit of CSR is a self-regulation process whereby you seek to integrate your stated corporate values and mission with your business model to ensure suitable ethical standards.

Needless to say, there is a lot of talk about CSR, but for some it is little more than window dressing – i.e. a lacklustre attempt to look like a business is doing the right thing. CRS analytics seeks to assess how aligned your words and your actions are when it comes to CSR.

Why does it matter?

Corporate social responsibility analytics matters because customers are much more discerning than they used to be. They have access to much more information than they used to and a business that behaves badly can rarely hide their actions for long. In the world of camera phones and social media, if a business behaves badly half the planet will know about it by lunchtime.

CSR is therefore morphing into a social licence to operate where your customers expect and will increasingly demand that you behave ethically, treat your workforce well and seek to limit your environmental impact. And if you don't, they will penalise you by shopping elsewhere.

When do I use it?

You need to conduct CSR analytics at least once a year.

If you are implementing any changes, shifting suppliers or have experienced bad publicity then you should measure this more often so you can gauge customer and public sentiment to ensure it is moving in the right direction.

What business questions is it helping me to answer?

Corporate social responsibility analytics helps you answer business questions such as:

- What impact does our business have on the social environment?
- To what extent do our customers appreciate our corporate social responsibility?
- Do our customers see us the way we want them to see us?

How do I use it?

Monitoring everything that is said about your business, products, services and brands can help you to assess how you are perceived by your customers and the wider community. This data can then be mined (Chapter 6) for insights that can help to improve decision making.

There are many tools and approaches that can help in your quest to measure your corporate social responsibility such as triple bottom line. Triple bottom line focuses on the three Ps – profit, people and planet.

Practical example

Being seen as a business that cares about its employees, the wider community, the planet and profit still has significant benefits for business in terms of PR and marketing opportunities.

In 2012, for example, Levi Strauss & Co were able to mitigate a corporate disaster not just for their brand reputation but also their profitability by committing to go toxic-free. Granted, the company's commitment came eight days after Greenpeace launched a report called 'Toxic Threads: Under Wraps' and screened a documentary about a family struggling to hold factories in Mexico to account for the pollution Levi and other international brands were causing.[1]

In the modern world with constant connectivity and social media, companies are no longer able to keep their poor behaviour under wraps. And companies that don't take their corporate social responsibility seriously enough will be penalised as customers become more informed and more discerning.

Tips and traps

CSR or the corporate social licence to operate is really important. All business has the potential to do a great deal of harm to the environment and the societies in which they operate but they can also be a genuine force for good. By assessing

---

[1]Klein, P. (2012) 'Three Ways to Secure Your Social License to Operate in 2013', *Forbes*, http://www.forbes.com/sites/csr/2012/12/28/three-ways-to-secure-your-social-license-to-operate-in-2013/

customer and public perception of your CSR you can ensure that you are consistently seen as the latter, not the former. And this does have an impact on revenue.

CSR can, however, be viewed as little more than 'green washing' so if you advertise your green credentials be very sure you can back them up. Even those committed to initiatives such as triple bottom line may find their commitment wavers in difficult economic times. It's easy to pay attention to people and the planet when profits are good – much tougher when the shareholders are complaining and your share price is dropping!

Further reading and references

To find out more about corporate social responsibility analytics see for example:

- http://www.iaia.org/iaiawiki/sia.ashx
- http://www.epa.gov/sustainability/analytics/social-impact.htm
- http://www.ibrc.indiana.edu/ibr/2011/spring/article2.html

What did you think of this book?

We're really keen to hear from you about this book, so that we can make our publishing even better.

Please log on to the following website and leave us your feedback.

It will only take a few minutes and your thoughts are invaluable to us.

www.pearsoned.co.uk/bookfeedback

Index